A List of FAIR Swanky Wages!

(The Equitable Wage System!)

By
The Worldwide People's Revolution!®

Book 065

(A Photo of a Pile of Money — P-6165)

A List of FAIR Swanky Wages!

Copyright Dedication and Introduction

By

Dr. Samuel Walker Edison, Ph.D., MA, BS, and QC!

ISBN — 13: 978-1537-3985-94

ISBN — 10: 1537-3985-98

00-01 [_] This Enlightening Book is COPYRIGHTED 2016—200016 AD, by **The Worldwide People's Revolution!**® All Rights are Reserved for **"The Swanky Associations of Working Soldiers,"** who will be Paid those Fair Swanky Wages for the Construction of **"GLORIOUS Swanky Hotels Castles and Fortresses!" (Beautiful Planned City States for WISE Intelligent Well-Educated People with Common Sense and Good Understanding!)**, which have more than 5,000 Advantages over normal Cities of Confusion, which are Destined to be TRASHED, after everything of Value has been Removed from them, in as much as that is Possible — such as Fine Furniture, Computers, TV's, Jewelry, Polished Marbles, Granites, Onyxes, Cookware, and especially well-made Tools — that is, Non-polluting Tools.

00-02 [_] No Portion of this Inspired Book shall be Reproduced by any Means for Sale without Written Permission from **The Worldwide People's Revolution!**® However, with their Permission, anyone in the World may Reproduce Exact Copies, and Sell them for a Reasonable Profit, and KEEP 90% of the Net Profits for their own Prosperity and Happiness: beCause **The Worldwide People's Revolution!**® only wants 10% of the Net Profits for the Construction of **"The Great World TEMPLE of PEACE,"** in Jerusalem, which will be the Tallest and Largest Building in the World, being nearly a Mile Tall and 8+ Miles in Diameter, which will be the Headquarters for **"The New RIGHTEOUS One-World Government,"** whose Stone Dome Home Complexes will be within that Great Temple — not only for the 6 High Priests from Major Religions; but, also for 60 Elected Kings from Major Nations, and 600 Elected Governors from Minor Nations and Islands of the Seas, plus our Great Elected King, who is the Inspired Author of more than 350 Unique Books, which contain Reasonable Solutions for our Massive Problems, which is WHY **The Worldwide People's Revolution!**® has Elected him to be that Great King: beCause, he alone has the Best Solutions, and Challenges anyone in the World to Present Better Solutions, for which he Offers a ONE-MILLION-DOLLAR REWARD!

00-03 [_] This Special Book is now DEDICATED to our Elected King, whose Name must be kept a Secret for the Present Time: beCause his Proposals are a Great Threat to the Evil Capitalist Empire, which has Managed to Produce a few so-called "Rich" People, who do not even have Fresh Clean Air to Breathe, Pure Living Water to Drink, nor Wholesome Natural Foods to Eat, let alone Secure Fireproof, Mouse-proof, Termite-proof, Hail-proof, Rot-proof, Paint-proof, Tornado-proof, Hurricane-proof, Earthquake-proof, Insurance-proof, and Self-air-conditioned Multi-million-dollar Stone Dome Home Complexes to Live in. Indeed, they are known as the 1%, who Share 95% of the Economic Pie, while the Remaining Tax Slaves, Interest Slaves, Insurance Slaves, Drug Slaves, Childcare Slaves, and Work Slaves are supposed to Share whatever is Left Over on their Proverbial Dinner Plates. Therefore, it is very easy to Understand WHY **The Worldwide People's Revolution!**® Strenuously Objects to that Hoggish

(The Equitable Wage System!)

Economic Plan, while they Observe the Masses of Poor People, who Suffer in their States of Extreme Poverty.

00-04 [_] For Example, not long ago there was a Great Flood of Water in Louisiana, whereby thousands of Houses and many Businesses were Flooded and Ruined to some Degree, if not Destroyed, while at the same Time more than a hundred Houses in Californicate were Transformed into Gray Ashes by Wild Fires — NOT beCause any God was Angry with any of those People; but, beCAUSE they were Ignorant FOOLS, as King Solomon would say, and as Jesus Christ Confirmed in his so-called *Sermon on the Mount,* when he said something like this:

A-[_] He who Hears these Inspired Sayings of mine with both of his Outer Ears and his Inner Ears, shall be Likened to a WISE Man, who Dug Down Deep into the Earth, and Built his House of Love on the Solid Bedrock of Divine Truths, which could by no Means be Destroyed: beCause it was Built Properly, in the Shape of a Stone Dome Home, much like the Pantheon in Rome, which will Endure for thousands of Years, being Self-air-conditioned, Fireproof, Termite-proof, Mouse-proof, Hail-proof, Rot-proof, Paint-proof, Tornado-proof, Hurricane-proof, Insurance-proof, and Tax-proof: because all of the Buildings, Highways, Bridges, Tunnels, Cisterns, Warehouses, Home-craft Workshops, Sales Shops, and Stone Dome Homes with Polished Marble Walls and Polished Granite Floors, belong to that Good GovernMint, which simply Mints and Prints the Necessary New Money for HIRING whomever is Willing and Able to Learn and Work, in Order to Help Build Beautiful Planned City States, which Stonework will Represent that New Money, which must be Earned by Honest Labor, without any Loans, without any Interest, and without any Taxes: beCause all of those Wise People Learn, Believe, Love, and Obey **the New MAGNIFIED Version of the Ten Commandments!**

B-[_] Therefore, Open your Spiritual Ears, and Listen Intently to me: beCause, he who Hears these Wise Sayings of mine, and does not Love nor Obey them, shall be Likened to an Ignorant Fool, who Built his House of Hate of the Shifting Sand Dune of Worldly Philosophies, which was Beat on by Driving Rains and Blowing Winds, which eventually Carried it Away, and Dumped it into the Sea of Forgetfulness, along with all of that other Trash! — Nigger Jim's Magnified Version (See *The Adventures of Huckleberry Finn and Tom Sawyer with Nigger Jim, Out Behind the Barn!* By Mark Twain, Junior.)

00-05 [_] So, O Doctor Samuel Walker Edison, do you actually have the Permission of your Elected King to use such Derogatory Words as "Nigger"?

00-06 [_] Well, our Elected King has his own Personal Definition of a "Nigger," which is quite Enlightening. {See www.Amazon.com for that Inspired Book, called: **"For the Love of Money!" (The Strange Things that People Say and Do to Get more Money!) By The Worldwide People's Revolution!®** Book 003.}

00-07 [_] So, O Doctor Edison, is it Fair to say that **The Worldwide People's Revolution!®** is a bit Crazy? After all, WHY are you Capitalizing so many of your Uninspired Words? Is that not INSANE? Indeed, even if it is not Insane, it is NOT Traditional; and therefore, it Upsets the Belly of my Mind, and Causes Great Spiritual Indigestion, you might say.

00-08 [_] Trust me, **The Worldwide People's Revolution!®** would not do anything without a Good Reason, which is WHY all such Words are Capitalized. {See **"Justifications for Capitalizations!" (WHY The Worldwide People's Revolution!® Defies the School of Fools by Capitalizing LOVE and HATE!), Book 049.**}

00-09 [_] O Doctor Edison, is it not WRong for us to HATE anyone or anything? Are we not supposed to LOVE everyone? Are you a Righteous Person, or a Wicked Person? And what about your Elected King, is he Righteous or Wicked?

00-10 [_] Well, if you Love Adultery, Stealing, Lying, Robbing, and Murdering, then that Love must be BAD; but, if you HATE Adultery, Stealing, Lying, Robbing and Murdering, then that Hate must be GOOD: beCause there is no Sane Person on this Earth, including yourself, who Objects to that Good Hate; nor who Condones that Evil Love, which is Proven every Day in Courtrooms around the World. Therefore, Love and Hate can be both Good and Evil. Indeed, it is my Hope and Prayer that you will Learn to LOVE ALL THAT IS GOOD, who is otherwise known as GOD; while you should Learn to HATE ALL THAT IS EVIL, who is known as Satan, the DEVIL!

00-11 [_] O Doctor Sam, I am already beginning to Fall in Love with YOU: beCause of the Beauty of your Simplicity, whereby you can make Complicated Things so Plain and Easy for us to Understand, while Jesus Christ made almost everything into a Bad Hair Day, as some People might say, whereby few of the Children can Understand it, even though it might be that Innocent Children can Understand many Spiritual Things that most Adults cannot Understand: beCause their Minds are Blinded by their Pride, which Kills their Good Understanding, you might say, whereby they cannot even Agree that it would be GOOD if almost all People in the World were Living in their own Small PANTHEONS, which everyone should Study in *Wikipedia,* which is Free of Charge. Indeed, those Silly "Adults" are Suffering with Chronic Constipation of their Minds with a Capital S and 2 C's, which can be Proven by having them Check the Appropriate Boxes below with X marks — that is, if they Agree with the Statements, they should Check those Boxes with X's.

>A-[_] I Agree that it would be Good if almost every Family in the World were Living in their own Private Pantheons, having Polished Marble Walls and Polished Granite Floors in a Stone Dome Home Complex, which would Include 4 large one-million-gallon Cisterns for Water Storage, a Luscious one-acre All-Mineral Organic Garden, which is 210 feet by 210 feet, which is Attached to their Spacious Walk-in Cooler / Freezer / Root Cellar Dome, which is Attached to their Spacious Kitchen, which is at least 20 feet in diameter, which is Attached to their Spacious Living Room, which is at least 24 feet in diameter, which is Attached by Stone Barrel-vault Tunnels to their Spacious Bedroom Domes, which are Attached to their Spacious Bathroom Domes and Storage Domes, which are Attached to their Home-craft Workshop Domes and Sales Shop Domes — all of which are Fireproof, Mouse-proof, Termite-proof, Hail-proof, Rot-proof, Paint-proof, Tornado-proof, Hurricane-proof, Insurance-proof, Self-air-conditioned, and Tax-proof!

>B-[_] I Believe that it would be Good for most People in the World to have such Well-made Houses and Gardens; but, I do not Believe that anyone could Afford to Buy such a House: beCause, just one of those Cisterns would Cost more than a Million Dollars! †‡

C-[_] I Confess that it would be a Good Idea to Think about it; but, it is Totally Impractical: beCause there is not enough Space on this Earth for every Family of 4 People to have a one-acre Garden, even if all of those Gardens are on the Roofs of all such Stone Dome Home Complexes: so that no Space is Wasted. †§‡

D-[_] Demon-ocracy would never Vote for it, even if there are a hundred Acres per Family in the World: beCause the Masses of People are far too Lazy to Work in all such Gardens and Home-craft Workshops, whereby they might Live and Work at HOME, or near Home, in someone else's Home-craft Workshop. Indeed, most People would Prefer to get up at 5 A.M., fix their Breakfast, Eat, Shower, Dress themselves, and Fight through the Traffic Jams for 2 Hours to get to Work at some Boring Job in a Factory or Office Building, where the Air Ducts are Filled with Bad Bacterias. And then, after that Slave Labor, they get to Enjoy Driving Home to their Wooden / Plastic Firetrap Mouse-infested Cockroach Dens with the Stinking Carpets, Dangerous Fiberglass Insulation, Toxic Termite Sprays, and all of those Healthy Happy Children, who have been Feasting on Chips and Dips that contain a thousand Capitalist Poisons, whereby they Weigh as much as Baby Walruses. †§‡§§

E-[_] Educated People know that Americans are FREE, and with a Capital F, whereby they can Choose to Breathe as much Fresh Crisp Clean Air as they Want to, even while Driving to Work on those Polluted Highways with their Brown Noses stuck up the Tailpipes of a thousand Cars. Yes, they are also Free to Eat Good Wholesome Natural Foods from the Gross Grocery Stores, except that not one in a hundred can Afford to Buy really Good Foods, even if they are for Sale. However, I Challenge you to Discover any Foods from the *Garden of Eden,* anywhere on the Earth. †§‡§§

F-[_] I Fail to Understand what this Survey is all about, which is Driving me Crazy!

G-[_] God Knows that you are being Driven Crazy by the EVILS of Capitalism, and not by the Provable Truths within this Inspired Book, which God Loves: beCause he Inspired it for his own Glory. Yes, every Good Thing Glorifies GOD, including the Pantheon, in Rome, which is a Good Example of a GOOD House. Do you Doubt that?

H-[_] HUMBUG! The Pantheon is far too Large for a Living Room. Indeed, it is 148 feet in Diameter, and also 148 feet from the Floor to the Ceiling, which has a large Hole in the Roof, which is big enough for a Car to pass through it, which lets in the Rain and Snow. ‡

I-[_] I Like Insurance Bills. Send all of the Bills to me: beCause I am NOT Insane! †§‡§§

J-[_] Justice Demands that the Author of this Insane Book should be brought to Trial for Tormenting us Americans: beCause we are the Freest People on the whole Earth, even if we are Tax Slaves, Interest Slaves, Insurance Slaves, Drug Slaves, Sex Slaves, Childcare Slaves, and Work Slaves: beCause we are Free to Run our Mouths, which is True Freedom: beCause it is Freedom of Speech, which, according to the Low Court of Supreme Injustices, is MONEY! Yes, Money is Freedom of Speech, they say; but, Freedom of Speech is NOT Money, or else we would have Unlimited Amounts of it, just for Talking and Talking. {See: **"The Washington Journal is a FARCE!"** Book 006.}

K-[_] King Jesus would not Live in the Pantheon, nor in any House that is like it: beCause it is full of Roman Idols, whom they Imagined were GODS! †§‡

L-[_] Lots of Laughs! King Jesus is now Living in a Beautiful Stone Dome Home Complex in Mount Zion, which is made from Solid ONYX of Multiple Colors. ‡ {See: **"The Secret City of the Great King!" (HOW the True Church will Escape from the Great Tribulation!) By The Worldwide People's Revolution!® Book 042.**}

M-[_] Jesus never had enough Money to Buy any such House. Therefore, Jesus could not be Living in any Onyx Stone Dome Home Complex, much less a SOLID Polished Onyx Dome that is 40 feet in Diameter! ‡

N-[_] You Religious People are NUTS! There is no Eternal City of the Great King. {See *Psalms 48, 50, and 87, King James Version (KJV)* for the Proof.} God is NOT known in her Palaces for a Refuge, which is a Place to Run and Hide during Times of Troubles.

O-[_] Are there no Options? Can we not Choose to Live in Mud Huts, Tarpaper Shacks, Bamboo Huts, Tin Sheds, or Igloos? I Prefer one of those Trailer Houses, like the ones that got Blown Away in that Tornado awhile back: because that Way I can Collect some Insurance, which might Cover one-quarter of the Cost of it. For Example, FEMA Awarded the Victims in Louisiana with 5,000$ for their 150,000$ Houses, if they did not have Flood Insurance, which was Better than nothing; but, it was certainly not enough Money for Buying another House of any Kind, except for one of those Lovable Used Trailer Houses, which might be big enough for 2 Dogs and a half-dozen Cats, which is a Better Option than an Igloo, which is made from Ice, which might Melt in a Day or 2, at least in Louisiana, in August, when it might be 110 °F! †§‡§§

P-[_] People have always been a bit Crazy; but, you People are Extremely INSANE! Why would you not Prefer to Build Adobe Houses in Arid-zona, where the Temperature might reach up to 120 °F, during the Daytime; but, the Nights are Guaranteed to be COOL at the Correct Elevation, which might even Freeze in June! Therefore, if the Adobe Walls are 4 feet THICK, they will Stabilize the Inside Temperatures of the House, which will Average about 72 °F, which is Perfect for Living in Riotous Pleasures, if you just Remember to set a Bottle of Fine Pistachio Wine outside before you go to Bed at Night, and then Remember to get up Early in the Morning to Close Up the Lid on the Cooler with the Wine, which will stay Cool all Day, if the Cooler is made Properly with a Foot of Insulation around Glass or Rocks or even Pottery. Indeed, I use Dry Chicken Feathers for Insulation, all of the way around the Stone Cooler, which is as big as a large Freezer, having a Door on the Top of the Box, which keeps all of my Foods and Drinks Cool, for FREE. †§‡

Q-[_] The Great Question is this: **"Do you Agree that it would be GOOD if almost everyone in the World were Living in Beautiful Swanky Stone Dome Home Complexes?"**

R-[_] Not even the Richest Romans could Afford to Buy such Houses. Therefore, the Question is Irrelevant to Reality.

(The Equitable Wage System!)

S-[_] That is a Different Subject. Try to Stick with the Subject — do you Agree that it would be GOOD if almost everyone in the World were Living in Beautiful SWANKY Stone Dome Home Complexes? [_] Yea, or [_] Nay?

T-[_] The Property Taxes would be more than anyone could Afford to Tally Up!

U-[_] You Fail to Understand that those are Different Subjects, which are not Relevant to the Great Question that is being Asked! For God's Sake, can you not Agree that it would be GOOD if almost everyone were Living in a Fireproof, Mouse-proof, Termite-proof, Hail-proof, Rot-proof, Paint-proof, Tornado-proof, Hurricane-proof, Tsunami-proof, Earthquake-proof, Self-air-conditioned, Insurance-proof HOUSE? [_] Yes, or [_] No?

V-[_] I am a Victim of Capitalism, who am far too Proud to Confess that my Wooden / Plastic Firetrap Mouse-infested Cockroach Den is a BAD House to Live in. Indeed, I LOVE my Insurance Bills, as well as the Constant FEAR that I might come Home to some Gray Ashes: beCause of some Professional Arsonists, who might take up a Different Kind of TERRORISM than America have ever Experienced. After all, we are Vulnerable to the Arsonists, who might carry it out with Drones that Drop Fire Bombs!

W-[_] We would Wish to God that it never Happens to YOU; but, if that is what is Required to make you come to your Right Senses, then so be it — may your Whole City of Confusion become Gray Ashes! Otherwise, maybe it will Require World War 3! †§‡

X-[_] X-amount of People cannot Understand the Beauty of Simplicity. Rabbits do not have Heating nor Cooling Bills to Pay: beCause they are Wise People, you might say, who take Advantage of the Good Earth, even as the Pantheon has had no Heating nor Cooling Bills in more than 1,800 Years! And neither has Saint Peter's Basilica: beCause it was Properly DESIGNED by Saint Michelangelo! Moreover, there are other Churches and Buildings in Europe that take Advantage of the Good Earth, and so can we. †§‡

Y-[_] That was a Good Idea during Yesteryears; but, nowadays, we are Wiser, whereby we have Endless Bills to Pay, which make us Happy! And I am also not Insane. †§‡§§

Z-[_] The Zeal of **The Worldwide People's Revolution!**® will Change your Mind, or else some Violent Storm will, or else World War 3 will; but, one Way or another, you will either Change your Mind, or else you will go to HELL, and Shovel Coal with the Devil, whom you Obviously Love. After all, just how Painful would it be to Confess that almost all of these American Houses are Potential DISASTERS, being Designed by Capitalist HOGS! Yes, the People who most Profited from them were Rich Bankers, Insurance Companies, Hardware Stores, Lumber Stores, Construction Workers, and People who did not Need any such EVIL Things for True Prosperity, even as Jesus Christ did not Need nor Want any of those Evil Things: beCause he Acted like the WISE Man, who Dug Down Deep and Built his Stone Dome Home on the Solid Bedrock of Divine Truths, which none of you Capitalists have Blown Away until this very Day. ‡

00-12 [_] I am not a Capitalist. I am also a Socialist. I Believe that Rich People should Share their Wealth with Poor People, even if they have to put their Fine Hand-crafted Furniture into the

Wood-burning Stove, just to keep from Freezing to Death: beCause of not having enough Common Sense to Build a PROPER HOUSE, which would have to be a Swanky Stone Dome Home Complex, like the Pantheon, to some Degree, except much smaller, and in several Domes, each of which would have a Skylight Hole in the Top of it for a Vent and Light, which would also be covered for Protection from Rains, Snows, Hailstones, Dust Storms, and even Bombs — that is, IF we cannot figure HOW to Establish **"The New RIGHTEOUS One-World Government,"** whereby we can get RID of all of those Hateful Bombs and Bullets: beCause they are not Needed for True Prosperity. However, if some Nation of Fools does Imagine that all such Bombs and Bullets are Needed, they can have ALL of them Dumped on their Heads! Yes, they can be BOMBED OFF of the Earth with Hydrogen Bombs! †§‡§§

00-13 [_] And is that something that you would Want some Wicked Nation to do to YOU, if your Wicked Federal Government did not Agree to get RID of all such Hateful Weapons? NO! Of course not! So, forget about doing any such EVIL Things. After all, our Elected King has a much Better Master Plan, which every Sane Person can Agree with, which will not Require any Hateful Wars: beCause he uses **"The Swanky Sword of Divine Truths!"** Yes, it is Extremely Sharp and Powerful, being the most Powerful Weapon in the World! Therefore, give yourself a Chance to Learn all about it and his Master Plan, which is Extremely GOOD, which is Inspired by GOD!

00-14 [_] O Doctor Edison, I can already Sense that this is an Exceptionally Good Book, which should be "red" aloud in all Churches, Mosques, Synagogues, Temples, Cathedrals, Basilicas, Theaters, Auditoriums, Concert Halls, Gymnasiums, Courtrooms, Prisons, Ball Parks, Funeral Homes, Businesses, Factories, and wherever People are Gathered Together.

00-15 [_] Well, by the Grace of God, **The Worldwide People's Revolution!®** will make that Happen; and you can do your Small but Meaningful Part by Selling Copies of this Inspired Book to whomever has Wisdom. However, Truly Wise People would Unite their Effort, Time, Money, Energy, and Materials. For Example, if a Church of 100 or more People Act Wisely, they will Buy a single Copy of this Inspired Book, and read it aloud to the entire Congregation, which will Satisfy their Souls much more than another Diarrhea of the Mind by some Irreverent LOUDMOUTH Slothgut Windbag Hole-in-Thy-Head, who has no Reasonable Solution for anything: beCause he is Related with those Political Rabbits in Washington, in the District of Criminals, who come Out of their Stinking Holes every few Years, and Hop all around the Country to give to us their Repetitious Political Speeches, which Promise Higher Wages, Lower Taxes, Better Security, Better Health Care, less Crimes, and Unity between White People and Black People, who are about as Compatible as Iron and Clay Mixed Up in a Stew Kettle with Snakes and Rats, which STINKS! Indeed, they would like us to Believe that People who are like Sheeps and Goats can get along Well with People who are like Lions and Wolves; but, it is just another Grand Deception and Red Jew LIE, which is not at all Biblical nor Truthful. Nevertheless, we must Confess that the Great American Experiment was Worth it, if we have at last Learned our Lessons, and are now Willing to Change our Ways of Thinking and Living! ‡

(The Equitable Wage System!)

The Enticing Menu for a Feast of Truths

Chapter 01 — What are "Swanky" Wages? ... page 10

Chapter 02 — Who can Afford to Pay Swanky Wages? ... 18

Chapter 03 — What is Wrong with the Welfare State? ... 28

Chapter 04 — More Nails in the Boards! ... 35

Chapter 05 — No more Debts ... 39

Chapter 06 — WHY the War on Poverty FAILED ... 42

Chapter 07 — Flushing Money Down the Drains! ... 48

Chapter 08 — A List of Swanky Wages for certain Kinds of Work ... 51

Chapter 09 — Arguments Against Fair Swanky Wages! ... 70

Chapter 10 — The Confusion of Dealing with Money ... 73

Chapter 11 — Working for the Fun of it! ... 83

Chapter 12 — The Price that People Pay for Rejecting Truths ... 87

Chapter 13 — There will be Peace in the Valley! ... 90

Chapter 14 — A Summary of my Master Plan ... 97

Chapter 15 — The Conclusion ... 101

Chapter 16 — Other Fascinating Literature by the same Inspired Author ... 105

The Enticement is on the Back Cover ... page 112

— Chapter 01 —

What are "Swanky" Wages?

01-01 [_] Well, after Doctor Samuel Walker Edison has raked over such Hot Burning Coals, and has Stirred Up such a Great Forest Fire of Truths — Consciously or Unconsciously — I am not Sure that I can Compete with him for Literary Artistic Flatteries; but, I will Try, if you will be Patient with me. After all, I am a Grade School Dropout, as they say; and therefore, there is only a Small Chance — as in one Book in a Million — that this one will be Successful, and so Successful that it will be one of the most Sold Books in all of History, just after: **"The New RIGHTEOUS One-World Government!" (HOW to Establish a Righteous One-World Government without Going to WAR!) By The Worldwide People's Revolution!®** Book 056.

01-02 [_] However, I have been Trying to Think of a Way whereby I might Provide this Inspired Book for FREE, now that most of my fellow Americans are so Poor that they can barely Feed and Clothe themselves without getting Food Stamps. Yes, **"The Great False Economy is now DEBUNKED!"** However, it has not yet been Laid to Rest with **"The UGLY Scarred Dishonest Face of Poor Old Miserable UNCLE SAM,"** who is now Looking Cross-eyed in the Mirror of Truths, if you know what I Mean: beCause he is so Confused by the FACTS. Indeed, he probably Skipped Over the Introduction to this Special Book, which is in Deed about WAGES; but, not just Ordinary Wages — such as 10 to 20 dollars per Hour — but, it is about First Class SWANKY Wages, which are no less than 10$ per Hour just to Babysit a Telephone, and 40$ per Hour to do Secretary Work in an Air-conditioned Office, and 50$ per Hour just to Hoe Weeds in an Organic Garden, and 60$ per Hour to Set Marble Tiles on the Solid Stone Walls of your own Beautiful Swanky Stone Dome Home Complex, GUARANTEED!

01-03 [_] Yes, you might say that such a Thing is IMPOSSIBLE! "Nobody could Afford to Pay such Wages," you might say. Well, in the Capitalist System, I would have to Agree with you: beCause, for Example, it would not even be Profitable to Build any of those one-million-gallon Cisterns for Water Storage, until the Rain should STOP; and then those Capitalist Weeping Willows would Spring Up and HOWL to the Federal Government to "PLEASE COME and HELP US!" Yes, like those Ignorant Poor People in Louisiana, who got Flooded Out by a 30-inch Rain, they would be BEGGING for Help from Big Daddy in Washington, who is only 20 Trillion Dollars in DEBT!

01-04 [_] Yes, that Debt is enough Money to reach half way to the Moon, if it were Stacked Up in 100$ Bills, back to back, and face to face, being Compressed, whereby 200,000$ equals one foot in the Stack, which you can Calculate for yourself, or otherwise Visit with one of my Inspired Books, called: **"The Divided States of United Lies!" (The so-called "United States of North America" in Disguise!) By The Worldwide People's Revolution!®**, Book 058, even though I am not Willing to BET that **that** Book is the one that Contains all of those Calculations: because I have not yet taken the Time to make up a Master Index for all of my Books, and I am far too Lazy to Open that Book in my Computer to Discover it; but, I am Willing to Bet that it does Mention that Important Subject in Chapter 05 of that Good Book, which is likely Repeated in some other Book: beCause I make a Habit of Repeating certain Important Information, if only with PART of the Full Details, whereby I am Deliberately Playing Tricks on the Foxes and Bloodhounds in the District of Criminals, in Washington, who will have to SEARCH and RESEARCH ALL of my Inspired Books, just to Try to come up with a Legal Case in a Courtroom, whereby they might have their Arguments Lined Up Against me. After all, I am at the very Top of their "Most Wanted" List, and NOT for Committing any Outlandish Crimes like those Lying Zionist Red Jew Banksters on Wall Street have Committed; but, for Upsetting the Great False Economy, if you can Believe it, which was doing Fine, they say, until that WICKED KING arose, who has been Elected by **The Worldwide People's Revolution!®**

01-05 [_] Yes, they are an Insignificant Voluntary Army of Working Soldiers, who have come to Understand that there is a Way to have **"Beautiful Swanky PALACES"** without having any Banks nor any Bankers, much less any Political Rabbits in Washington, District of Corruption: beCause the only Thing that is Needed is **"The New RIGHTEOUS One-World Government,"** which will be Established by Jesus Christ, if not by me, who has come to Prepare the Way for his Second Coming! Yes, many of my Readers will Automatically Know Exactly WHO I AM, now that I have let that "Cat Out of the Bag," as they say. However, Believe it or not, many of those Politicians will have no Idea WHO I AM: beCause they have not Studied that Ancient Book, called the *Holy Bible,* which is not so HOLY as you might Imagine: beCause it was Mutilated by Lying Zionist Red Jews, who call themselves Jews; but, they are of the Synagogue of SATAN, even as Jesus said, who was not Lying by any Means. (See *Revelation 2:9 and 3:9, KJV.*)

01-06 [_] Now, if you just Happen to be one of those Zealous Professing "Christians," you might say something like this: "I know for a fact that the Holy Bible is the pure word of God, without any errors, even if there are 200+ Versions of it: because they are all in perfect agreement with Buzzeldick the Great, who is the God of the Prosperity Gospel." Yes, I am being very Sarcastic; but, not without Good Reasons. Please Notice that you did NOT say, "I Know for a Fact with a Capital K and F that the Holy Bible in the *King James Version* is made up of the Pure Words of the Living God, being without any Errors, which is WHY the *King James Version* has no less than 10,000 *Italicized Words* to Enhance it, without which the Books would not even be Understandable." No, you did not Confess that those 200+ Versions have Legitimate Reasons for Correcting all such Mistranslations as one might Discover in the other Versions. Trust me, the Translators all Agree 100% that there is no such a Thing as *"the Pure Words of the Living God,"* in ENGLISH, when he Spoke in Hebrew, Greek, Aramaic, Babylonian, Phoenician, or in some other Language; but, certainly NOT in Elizabethan English, which was not even Invented until the 1600's! Therefore, the "Purity" of all such Mistranslations is Recognized by all Honest Translators as Pure NONSENSE: beCause of the "Impossibility of Translating one Language into another Language," in its so-called "Purity." However, if you Doubt it, just Ask a Linguist, who will quickly tell you that English and Spanish, for Example, are as Different as Horses and Burros, which may Look somewhat Alike; but, they most Definitely have Contrary Personalities, even as Mexicans are by Nature much Different than Canadians and Hindus from India.

01-07 [_] So, just Exactly what are First Class Quality *Swanky* Wages? Can we have Total Fairness with any Kind of Wages for any Kind of Goods or Services? For Example, one Healthy Happy Ambitious Young Person might Hoe 10 Times more Weeds in the Garden than some Sick Depressed Gloomy Poisoned Person, who has no Heart in it, who would rather just DIE, than Work: beCause of being a Victim of Capitalism! ‡

A-[_] I Agree that a Person's Feelings and Attitude toward something can make all of the Difference in how Well something gets Done. For Example, there was once a Visionary Teenager, who got the Bright Idea that he and his new Girlfriend could Plant an Acre of Cantaloupes on her Dad's Farm by their own Labor: because they had all of the Necessary Tools to Work with, whereby they could Earn no less than 2,000$ for no more than 2 Weeks of Work: beCause those Cantaloupes were Selling at the Farmer's Market for 1$, each. However, in this Case, they were very Blest to have a very Large 5-acre Garden, whereby they could make just 2 Long Rows, 400 feet long, and thus provide more Space for the Cantaloupe Vines to SPREAD OUT, which they Naturally did; but, not until that Young Couple went to WORK with their Shovels and Hoes, and Mounded Up the Dirt 2 feet High for the full length of those 2 Rows, whereby the Dirt got lots of AIR Mixed in with it, which, like Magic, seemed to Fertilize it: beCause they also Mixed into that Topsoil no less than 5 Tons of Compost per Row, which Required a LOT of Sweating, even during the Springtime, even during the Early Morning Hours of each Day, which they were Happy to do: beCause they were in LOVE! Yes, it always Helps to be in Love with someone, which is Greatly Enhanced with a Thing called HOPE! Indeed, they had Great Hopes in their Hearts, whereby they were going to Prove that one does not have to Buy a 120,000$ Tractor, just to Grow 2,000-dollars-worth of Sweet Fragrant Cantaloupes with only 2 Weeks of Hard Work, and a few Tons of Compost, and a few Seeds, which were all Planted during just one Day, in less than 2 Hours! Yes, the Planting of the Seeds was the Least of the Work, which is WHY the Women Pioneers Planted the Seeds in the Gardens that their Husbands Prepared for them: beCause those Men did 99% of the Work to get those Gardens Prepared, even if NOT by **"The LUSCIOUS All-Mineral Organic Method of Gardening!" (HOW to Grow DELICIOUS Satisfying Foods for Potential Kingz and Kweenz in Swanky PALACES!) By The Worldwide People's Revolution!® Book 021.** Therefore, most all Pioneer Women were Happy to Attend to their Cooking and Knitting and Planting Seeds in their Gardens. However, in this Case, the Young Lady most likely did more Work than her Potential Husband: beCause she just Naturally had more LOVE than he had, and thus more Ambition. Nevertheless, it is Fair to say that he also did a LOT of Hard Work to get those Long Rows Prepared in that Large Garden: beCause we are talking about Moving no less than 20 Tons of Dirt in each Row: beCause each Row Required that they first of all Dig Up the Topsoil in each Row, and Mix that Compost into it, and then Rake or Shovel the nearby Topsoil into each Row, in order to make LONG MOUNDS of Dirt to Plant those Seeds in, whereby the Roots of the Plants would not be Drowned Out by Sitting in Water, just in Case it Happened to Rain too much, whereby the Garden might be Flooded: beCause it was Located in "Bottom Land," which was as Flat as a Pancake for the most Part. Therefore, if the Dirt was RAISED UP, the Rainwater could Drain Off of it, and the Plants would not be Killed by too much Water on their Roots. Well, to make a Long Story Short, the Work got Done, and the Plants Grew and GREW, and Spread themselves OUT over an Acre of Land with Long Vines, which were Loaded with Cantaloupes! And then along came one of those Capitalist Acid Rains during one Dark Summer Night, like a Thief or an Enemy during the Night, which Caused all of those Vines to be Weakened by it, which Caused all of them to get a certain Disease, just when those Cantaloupes were within ONE WEEK of Harvest Time! Yes, it is a True Story; and you can Believe it: beCause I would not Lie to you about a Thing like that, for which there are several Witnesses, who will be Happy to Testify in a Courtroom, if anyone Doubts it. So, the

(The Equitable Wage System!)

Bottom Line is this — not one Cantaloupe was Harvested nor Sold; but, all of them went to Waste: beCause they were not Fit to Eat — Thanks to that Acid Rain, which was Caused by those "Beloved" Gasoline-powered Vehicles, and those Capitalist Factories, which Spew Out Toxic Dung into the Air, which is only Loved by Ignorant FOOLS: beCause it is Possible and most Practical for everyone to be Living in **"Beautiful Swanky PALACES,"** and without any Stinking Noisy Polluting Abominations! ‡

B-[_] I do not Believe it.

C-[_] I Confess that it might be True.

D-[_] I Doubt that it is True; but, for the Sake of Learning a Good Lesson, I will Play along with the Story: beCause it is also Doubtful that any Intelligent Human Being would go to all of the Trouble to Write such a Book as this without Good Reasons — one of which is to Teach Young People that they should not get their Expectations too High in the Capitalist World, lest they should Break their own Hearts. Indeed, there were many other Things that could have Ruined that Cantaloupe Crop, even if the Acid Rain had Failed: beCause there are certain Creatures that Love to Eat on all such Plants, not to Mention a Multitude of Diseases, Insects, Raccoons, Opossums, and Cut Worms, which neatly Snip Off the Plants just above the Ground Level: beCause they are Inventions of the Devil, himself! Yes, the Devil is in the Details, you might say: beCause that is the Nature of Things in this World of Woes, which has been Damned to Hell by some Strange God, who could just Suddenly Appear in the Dark Awesome Rolling Clouds of a FEARSOME Sky, along with tens of thousands of his Flying Saucers, and put on a Night Show like People have never Seen before! Yes, the entire Sky could be Transformed into a Large TV Screen, all around the World, whereby the History of Mankind could be Shown since the Days of Adam and Eve in the Garden of Eden, and in all Languages; but, such a Thing is Unrealistic, and only a Religious DREAM, you might say. †§‡

E-[_] Educated People Know for a Fact that those Young People had all of the Faith, Hope, Love, Trust, Patience, Persistence and Obedience that was Necessary for Producing a Good Crop of Cantaloupes, which could have easily Sold for 2$ each: beCause of their Sweet Fragrance and Size, whereby just one Smell would Sell an entire Bushel Basket of them to any Nolijuboul Customer, who would put that Bushel Basket in his or her Walk-in Cooler, whereby he or she might Eat one such Cantaloupe per Day for an entire Week, which would be the Highlight of the Day, which would be Better than Kisses that are Sweeter than Wine. Yes, such Sweet Fragrant Cantaloupes would Light the Fire of True Love in any Heart that might get to Share them with someone they Love; but, behold, it Turned into Bitterness and Endless Regrets, just to Think about it. †§‡

F-[_] I Fail to Understand WHY the Father did not Warn his Daughter to not get her Hopes Worked Up too High, seeing that it was just 3 Years before that when that same Garden got a similar Acid Rain on no less than 5,000 Tomato Plants, which Suffered the same Fate! Yes, it is a True Story — all of those Plants DIED, Thanks to Capitalism! ‡

G-[_] God Knows that it is a True Story; but, the Great Question is this: **"HOW can such Evil Things be STOPPED?"** Did those Young People not have any Farmer's Insurance, whereby they could have been Paid for their Losses of Time, Money, Materials, and Energy? Whatever Happened to JUSTICE and EQUAL RIGHTS for EQUAL Wages for Equal Services?

H-[_] I Honestly have no Idea WHY anyone would take such Chances to Plant anything in a Garden, seeing that the Whole Earth is CURSED by Capitalism, which should be Hanged to the nearest Tree, until DEAD! ‡

I-[_] If those Young People had had CROP INSURANCE, they would not have Suffered for it, which would have only Costed them $199.98 for those 2 Rows of Cantaloupes, whereby they could have Collected at least 400$: beCause that would be the Expected Production of 2 such Rows of Cantaloupes in a Normal Garden. However, in such an Ideal Situation, with such Fertile Land and Convenient Compost: beCause of having Livestock on the Farm, one can Expect a Bumper Crop like that. Yes, it is Possible to Produce as many as 10,000 Cantaloupes from 2 Rows that are 400 feet long, if the Plants are Close Together, and the Seeds are Planted 6-inches apart in 2 Rows that are one-foot apart in each of those Long Rows, for a Total of 4 Rows, whereby each Row has no less than 1,600 Plants, or a Total of 3,200 Plants in both Long Rows, each of which might Produce 3 or 4 Cantaloupes per Vine, even though the World Record is something like 20 Cantaloupes per Vine during one Season: beCause of having very GOOD Topsoil, according to: **"The LUSCIOUS All-Mineral Organic Method of Gardening!"** Therefore, it was not an Unrealistic Expectation for that Young Couple, whose Insurance should have Covered no less than 20,000$ in that Case: beCause they had Piles of Cantaloupes to be Inspected by the Insurance Agent for the Proof. †§‡

J-[_] Justice Demands that the Federal Government should be Responsible for all such Crop Failures: beCause they are the Unholy Ones who Allowed those Capitalist Hogs to Produce those Abominations that Caused the Acid Rains. Therefore, they should Insure all such Crops: so as to not Discourage any more Young People from going to Work. ‡

K-[_] Are you Kidding? There is no Government on this Earth that could Afford to Reimburse People for such Great Losses. However, if they could Afford it, all of the Young People in the World would be Digging Up the Land, and Planting Cantaloupes: beCause, who would not Want to Earn 20,000$ for only 2 Weeks of Hard Work, which could be done with an Old Used Tractor, or even with 2 large Mules and some Proper Tools, like the Old Older of Mennonites do it. Yes, I would Personally Plant no less than 10 such Rows of Cantaloupes in my own Garden: beCause that would be a Total of 100,000$ for only one Week of Work with a Tractor, even though I am Sure that some Farmers could Accomplish it in only 2 Days, and maybe Plant 10 Times that much, and thus Collect 1,000,000$ from the Government Insurance: beCause all such Crops are almost Guaranteed to FAIL: beCause of those Capitalist Acid Rains! †§‡

L-[_] Lots of Laughs! No Government on the Earth would be so Foolish as to Insure all such Crops, after Learning about those Acid Rains. However, if our Elected King had his Way, those Government Officials would have to Demonstrate HOW to Grow a Successful Crop of Cantaloupes in such Gardens, whereby they might come to Understand the NEED for Crop Insurance for Small Farmers, which is NOT now

(The Equitable Wage System!)

Available to any of them: beCause of the above mentioned Reasons. Indeed, it is not Profitable for Insurance Companies; and therefore, it would most Certainly not be Profitable for the Federal Government to get into that Insurance Business, even though it is their Responsibility to Protect and Defend and Provide for the Common Welfare of the People, according to our Constitution, which Naturally Includes ALL Farmers, Large or Small, Rich or Poor, for Better or for Worse, in Good Times and in Bad Times, in Sickness and in Health: beCause the Federal Government is MARRIED to its People, which is WHY they Established it to begin with! Therefore, any Good Government would Protect its People, and Especially its Farmers: beCause, without those Farmers, we could all Starve to Death! Therefore, the Federal Government should do its Best to make Sure that all Farmers are Successful, even if it is a bit Expensive at Times, which Expenses could be Greatly Reduced by Constructing those **"GLORIOUS Swanky Hotels Castles and Fortresses!" (Beautiful Planned City States for WISE Intelligent Well-Educated People with Common Sense and Good Understanding!) By The Worldwide People's Revolution!®** Book 019.

M-[_] It is forever a Lack of MONEY in all such Cases, which must be Collected from TAX SLAVES, who cannot Afford such HIGH Taxes. †‡

N-[_] NONSENSE! That same Wicked Anti-Christ False Cover-up Federal government can and does Afford to WASTE no less than a Trillion Dollars per Year on so-called "Health Care": beCAUSE the Masses of People are not Eating those Good Sweet Fragrant Cantaloupes, which one cannot even Discover in the Gross Grocery Stores: beCause no one is Growing them! Therefore, the Masses of People are SICK: beCause of Eating Unnatural Unhealthy Foods. Therefore, that Government should get its Priorities in Order. {See www.Amazon.com for: **"HOW to Get our PRIORITIES in ORDER!" (The Glories of Democracy; and, Does DEMON-ocracy have its Priorities in Order?) By The Worldwide People's Revolution!®** Book 060.}

O-[_] There is another Option, which is called SOCIALISM, whereby the Wealth is taken away from Saint Peter to Pay Saint Paul, which is Equally as Unfair as Communism, which makes Slaves of almost everyone, and most Certainly Depresses almost everyone: beCause of Losing Hope in a Better World. Indeed, if you Want to Study a Classic Case of Socialism, just go to Greece, where one in 4 People are Working for the Government!

P-[_] One in 5 People in America are also Working for the Government, either for the Federal Government, the State Government, the County Government, or the City Government — all of which are in Debt up to their Necks — Thanks to Capitalism, which has Produced X-amount of Rich Gangster Banksters in New Yuck City and Lungdung, England; but, the Masses of People still INSIST that they are the Freest People in the World, in spite of being nothing but Tax Slaves, Interest Slaves, Insurance Slaves, Drug Slaves, Childcare Slaves, and WORK SLAVES! Yes, the Pumpkinheads will never Learn the Truth about themselves: beCause they have no BRAINS! †§‡

Q-[_] The Great Question is this: **"Is it Possible and Practical to Establish "The New RIGHTEOUS One-World Government," which has EQUAL WAGES for EQUAL SERVICES?"**

R-[_] I Reckon that it is Possible and most Practical; but, only IF it were Possible to get the Attention of the Tax Slaves, Interest Slaves, Insurance Slaves, Drug Slaves, Sex Slaves, and Work Slaves, who have been Sold Down the River with Poor Nigger Jim, who have no Idea HOW to Free themselves from all such SLAVERY by the Power of REGENERATION! Yes, it is a Religious Subject, you might say; but, it is one that Desperately Needs to be STUDIED with a Capital S: beCause it is Possible for those Sick Degenerated Children to be HEALED, just by Eating Wholesome Natural Foods and Drinks, instead of that Capitalist GARBAGE, which is not Fit to Feed to Hogs! Yes, it can be and must be Proven at: **"The Great Worldwide TELEVISED Court HEARING,"** when all such Subjects must be put on TRIAL. (See Chapter 16-041.) ‡

S-[_] I have Studied a LOT of Books during my Long Life, and I must Confess that **The Worldwide People's Revolution!®** is Miles Ahead of the Remainder of us Slaves, when it comes to Escaping from the Lying Zionist Red Jew TRAP, which is otherwise known as "The Military Industrial Congressional Bankers' Complex Economic System," which is more Thoroughly Discussed in: **"The PRAYERS of Pumpkinheads!"** Book 007. Yes, it goes into Details that are a bit Em-bare-assing to **"The UGLY Scarred Dishonest Face of Poor Old Miserable UNCLE SAM,"** who is Long Overdue for a Facelift and some Clean Clothing, after Wallowing around in the Slime Pits of Egypt with those Lying Red Jews, as Moses might say, who Commanded us to have a Year of JUBILEE, once every 50 Years, whereby all Debts must be Forgiven, and all of the Land must be Returned to the People, whereby each Family has no less than one whole Acre of Land for Growing their own Foods, whereby they do not have to be Standing in Long Soup Lines, nor at Welfare Offices with Drunkards, Prostitutes, Gluttons, nor Fools! ‡ (See *Leviticus 25, New KJV*.)

T-[_] Time has Proven Moses to be Correct; and that Great Year of Jubilee is Long Overdue by at least 2,000 Years! Therefore, it is now Time to Elect a RIGHTEOUS King to Govern us, whereby all Forms of Slavery can be brought to an END! Yes, **"Terrorists Beware that your Days are Numbered!" (HOW to Bring those Terrorist Attacks to a Screeching HALT!), Book 043.** {See **"Are we Tax Slaves of a Lower Order than Lying Red Jews?" (HOW to be Liberated from all Slavery, Worldwide!) By The Worldwide People's Revolution!® Book 052.**}

U-[_] I Understand what you are saying, and I Agree 100% that it would be Good if all People had one-acre All-Mineral Organic Gardens to Work in: beCause I have "red" an Inspiring Book, called: **"Poverty Hunger Riots Strikes Brutalities Election Deceptions and Civil Wars!" (The High Price that we Earthlings have Paid for Leaving the Good Land!) By The Worldwide People's Revolution!® Book 014.**

V-[_] Queen Victoria would Agree with you; but, I much Prefer to "reed": **"Are Americans the Most STUPID People who ever Lived?" (HOW Working People can PROSPER and Live in PEACE Under the Rulership of a RIGHTEOUS KING!) By The Worldwide People's Revolution!® Book 047.**

W-[_] Americans are so Stupid that they would Prefer to Fight in World War 3, rather than get up and go to Work at Home, in their own Gardens, Vineyards, Orchards, and

(The Equitable Wage System!)

Home-craft Workshops and Sales Shops within those **"GLORIOUS Swanky Hotels Castles and Fortresses,"** which just Happen to have more than 5,000 Good Reasons and Great Advantages for Building them and Living within the Borders of them! Indeed, they are not even Willing to Study all such Inspired Books: beCause they have their Heads Stuck Up the Tailpipes of Red Jew Capitalists, who Invented a very Good Economic System for themselves; but, NOT for us Tax Slaves, Interest Slaves, Insurance Slaves, Drug Slaves, Childcare Slaves, nor Work Slaves, who are Stuck with the BILLS to Pay, who Live in Fears from Day to Day, who have no Assurance of anything — except that we are Guaranteed to get Old, and DIE — Thanks to the Nature of Things, which was all Arranged by the Synagogue of SATAN, who Inspired that Unholy Mutilated Bible, which is Misinterpreted to say that we are all going to Heaven when we Die, which is nothing but a Red Jew LIE: beCause Jesus said, *"NO MAN HAS ASCENDED UP TO HEAVEN ..." — KJV of John 3:13,* which is the Gospel TRUTH! ‡

X-[_] X-amount of People have no Idea what you are Talking about, O Elected King; but, there is Coming a Great Tribulation, when all Souls will be Tested to the Maximum Amount for their Goodness. Therefore, it is not a Time to Act like FOOLS; but, to Act like WISE Men, who Work Together by United Effort to Save themselves, even as Noah and his Family Worked Together, or else they would have all Perished with the Unbelievers. ‡ {See: **"God Speaks and the Whole World Listens!" (Fire on the Mountain from the Burning Bush by the Spirit of Truth!)**, Book 026, plus: **"The Seven Basic Spiritual Building Blocks of LIFE!" (Faith Hope Trust Love Patience Persistence and Obedience!) By The Worldwide People's Revolution!®** Book 036.}

Y-[_] I am Yearning for the Day of Rest, when the Whole Earth is Living in Peace for a thousand Years, when Jesus Christ will Govern this World of Wonders in a State of Righteousness in Holiness, just as the *Holy Bible* Teaches. Yes, *"Blest are the Meek, Teachable People: because they will Inherit the Earth, not Heaven: because the Kingdom of God is Coming to the Earth, whereby the Will of God will be Done on the Earth, even as it is now Done in Heavenly Places,"* as Jesus might say: beCause, *"The Earth was Created for Mankind, while the Heavens were Created for the Godkind,"* as King David might say. Yes, Jesus went to Prepare a Place for his Holy Bride in the Hollow Earth, in Mount Zion, which is the Holy City of the Great King, which is otherwise known as *"the Secret Place of the Most High God,"* which has been Hidden from the Eyes of Mockingbirds and Fools for thousands of Years: beCause God Wanted to Test our FAITH, Hope, Trust, Love, Patience, Persistence and OBEDIENCE! Therefore, I Yearn for the Glad Day when we can all Sit under our Fruit Trees in Swanky Easy Chairs, and Listen to the little Birds of Cheerfulness Singing, while the Fragrant Flowers are Blooming, and the Happy Children are Playing in Peace. ‡ {See: **"The Secret City of the Great King!" (HOW the True Church will Escape from the Great Tribulation!) By The Worldwide People's Revolution!®** Book 042.}

Z-[_] The Zeal of **The Worldwide People's Revolution!®** will bring it to pass.

01-08 [_] O Elected King, I am Dumbfounded by all such Thoughts, which are mostly Strange Words to me, even though I do Understand the Meanings of the Words; but, NOT the Meanings of the Thoughts, which have me Confused.

01-09 [_] Trust me, it is your Vain Traditions that have you Confused — NOT my Inspired Words of Provable Truths.

01-10 [_] O King of the Birds, if we Elect you to be our Righteous King, we can all Immediately go to Work for Good Swanky Wages, Building **"The Environmentalists' Paradise"** for everyone who is Willing to Join **"The Swanky Associations of Working Soldiers!" (A Fascinating Collection of Various Kinds of Voluntary Working Soldiers!) By The Worldwide People's Revolution!® Book 018.**

— Chapter 02 —

Who can Afford to Pay Swanky Wages?

02-01 [_] Granted, very few Capitalists would be Willing to Pay Swanky Wages: beCause they would quickly put themselves Out of Business at the Rate of 60$ per Hour for Setting Polished Marble Tiles on Solid Stone Walls — unless we Adopted a NEW Economic System, whereby **"The New RIGHTEOUS One-World Government"** does it Work, which is the Work of HIRING **"Seven Great Armies of Working Soldiers"** to Help Build those **"GLORIOUS Swanky Hotels Castles and Fortresses,"** which have never been Built in this World of Woes: beCause, if they were Built for almost everyone in the World, HOW would those Lying Zionist Red Jews Obtain Trillions of Dollars by Banker-craft? Indeed, there would be no Need for any Bankers, nor for any Loans from **"The New RIGHTEOUS One-World Government,"** which would simply Mint and Print the Necessary Brand New Money with New Faces and Numbers for HIRING you and me and everyone else who might Want to Live in **"Beautiful Swanky PALACES,"** to Help Build them. Yes, the Stonework would Represent that New Money, which would have to be Earned by Honest Labor, without any Loans, without any Interest, and without any Taxes; but, only with VOLUNTARY TITHES and OFFERINGS! — that is, IF those **"Seven Great Armies of Working Soldiers"** just Happened to LOVE their New Government enough to Support them, which I Believe that they will: beCause of going from "Rags to Riches," as they say. Yes, within just 6 Years of Labor, most of the People in the World will be Living in those **"GLORIOUS Swanky Hotels Castles and Fortresses!" (Beautiful Planned City States for WISE Intelligent Well-Educated People with Common Sense and Good Understanding!) By The Worldwide People's Revolution!®** Book 019. After all, their Standard of Living would be Raised by no less than 100 Times! ‡

>A-[_] I Agree. I would Gladly Pay a Tithe of 10% of my Income for the Management of **"The New RIGHTEOUS One-World Government!" (HOW to Establish a Righteous One-World Government without Going to WAR!),** Book 056, whose Headquarters should be in **"The Great World TEMPLE of PEACE!" (The Glory of Jerusalem Arises Again!) By The Worldwide People's Revolution!®** Book 017.

(The Equitable Wage System!)

B-[_] I do not Believe it. Nobody would Pay any Tithes, much less any Offerings to a WICKED One-World Government, which would be telling each Planned City State HOW to Manage itself, and Ordering its Young Men to Join some Bloody Army of Murderous Soldiers, whereby New Yuck City could be Attacking Chicago and Lost Angels, Californicate. §§ {See: **"Does a Good Soldier have to be a MURDERER?"**}

C-[_] Can you Think of any Circumstances that would Call for the People of New York City to be Attacking Chicago and Los Angeles, California?

D-[_] Dimwitcrats and Reprobates would take Advantage of DUMBmocracy, whereby those Lying Zionist Red Jews would figure out HOW to make War by one Means or another: beCause they are the Chief Weapons Manufacturers, Bomb Makers, Chemists, Medical Doctors, and so on. Indeed, if it has Money Involved in it, those Red Jews are in the Midst of it, just like Jesus said: *"You are of your Evil Stepfather, the Devil; and therefore, the Lusts of your Father you will Fulfill. Indeed, he was a Murderer from the Beginning, and Lived not According to the Truth: because there is no Truth in him. Therefore, when he Speaks a Lie, he Speaks from his Heart: because his Heart is Set on Lies: because he is a Liar, and the Father of all Lies, who cannot be Trusted." — The New MAGNIFIED Version (NMV) of John 8:44.*

E-[_] That is very Enlightening to the Mind, O Elected King. Therefore, I must Read it once again with a Capital R, as in Carefully, Prayerfully, and Thoughtfully.

F-[_] I Fail to Understand WHY New York City would be Wanting to Attack Chicago and Los Angeles, just beCAUSE of Establishing **"The New RIGHTEOUS One-World Government!" (HOW to Establish a Righteous One-World Government without Going to WAR!) By The Worldwide People's Revolution!® Book 056.**

G-[_] God Knows for a Fact that it would never Happen, unless Satan was in Charge, and somehow Managed to Establish a WICKED One-World Government with Lying Zionist Red Jews in Charge of it, rather than Honest White Jews, like our Elected King.

H-[_] HUMBUG! There is no such a Creature as a RIGHTEOUS King, who does what is Right for ALL of the People: beCause all Men are Overcome by their Lusts for more and more MONEY! Indeed, if it were not True, WHY would your Elected King be SELLING his Inspired Books, which could be Provided *Free of Charge* on the Internet? †§‡

I-[_] You are Ignorant. Our Elected King Posted 314 Inspired Books on the Internet for everyone to Study, free of charge, and for 20+ Years; and not one Person sent to him a Dime for his Support, for Paying for the Website, which was more than a thousand dollars per Month. Indeed, even until this very Day, *Wikipedia* must BEG for Money: because most People are SELFISH and STINGY, who will not Support any Good Cause without someone BEGGING for Help, which is beneath the Dignity of our Elected King, who is NOT a Beggar of any Kind. Moreover, he does not Care whether or not People Choose to be Liberated from their Prison of Lies, or go on Suffering in the Darkness of Ignorance: beCause they Willing Choose to Waste their Hard-earned Money on TRASH and Garbage Foods, and do not even Complain about it. Therefore, if they are not Willing

19

to Spend some Money on some Inspired Books, to Hell with them! For Example, this Book Costs less than a small Meal at the Death and Hell Restaurant, and you can Feast on this Book all Day long, unto the Satisfaction of your Soul, while that Meal of Hog Slop or Dog Food will not Satisfy your Spirit, and might even make you Hungrier: beCause it is Loaded with Addictive Chemicals and Poisons, which can easily be Proven in a Courtroom. However, just take a Good Look at the People on the Streets, who are the Healthiest People among us, whose Fat Relatives are often too Fat to even get Out of their Houses! Therefore, it is Obvious that they are Starving to Death, even while Eating enough to Feed 3 Hogs! †§‡

J-[_] Justice Demands that all such People should Hear the Truths about Foods and Drinks, whereby they might make Rational Decisions concerning what should or should not be Eaten and Drank.

K-[_] King Jesus said that we can Eat anything that is found for Sale: because it is not that which Enters into our Mouths that Defiles us; but, it is that which comes Out of our Mouths — such as that VOMIT that you Preach, which was Inspired by Satan. †‡§§

L-[_] Lots of Laughs! King Jesus said, *"Except an Unclean Man should Humble himself by Means of Fasting and Praying, until he becomes like an Innocent Child with a Pure Mind and a Clean Body, both Inside and Outside, he shall in no Way Enter into the Holy Kingdom of All that is Good." — The Gospel According to Saint Bartholomew* ‡

M-[_] Money can Buy Good Health, which is WHY Howard Hughes was the Healthiest Happiest Person who ever Lived: because he Spent most of his Billions of Dollars on Medical Doctors and Magic Cures, which could not even Save Steve Jobs, who Died with Cancers. And I am Crazy; but, not Totally Crazy. †§‡§§

N-[_] NONSENSE! Neither Money nor Drugs ever Cured anyone: beCause it is the Natural Power of the Body to Heal itself. Therefore, once the Body has Lost that Power, that Body cannot be Healed without a Miracle from God, who is not Willing that anyone should Suffer; but, when we Reject his Natural Dietary Laws, HOW can he Help us? ‡ {See www.Amazon.com for: **"Did God or Satan Ordain Medical Doctors??" (Ask Huck Finn and/or Nigger Jim: because neither Tom Sawyer nor Judge Thatcher would Know!) By The Worldwide People's Revolution!® Book 022.**}

O-[_] It is my Honest Opinion that the Author of these Inspired Books is GOD, himself. ‡

P-[_] Many Ignorant People will be Imagining all such Vain Things, in spite of the Fact that there is no Truth in it: beCause the Author of these Inspired Books is just as Mortal as any of us, and may also Die from a Broken Heart, if his Good Books are Rejected by a Deceived Society of Professing "Christians," who have no Idea what it Means to be HOLY, even as Moses, Elijah, Jesus and John were Holy. {See: **"HOW to Become a HOLY Man!" (40 Good Reasons WHY People Should FAST and PRAY!) By The Worldwide People's Revolution!® Book 045, which is a Companion Book of: "The Proper RULES for FASTING!" (The Complete Instruction Manual for True Repentance!), Book 046.**}

(The Equitable Wage System!)

Q-[_] The Great Question is this: **"Will the Bride of Christ be Ready for the Wedding of the Nations when their Master Returns?"** {See: **"The END of CONFUSION!" (The Great CELEBRATION of the Magnificent Wedding of the Humble Honest Nations, and the Grand Year of JUBILEE!) By The Worldwide People's Revolution!®** Book 050.

R-[_] I am Ready.

S-[_] I Stink from my Stinking Feet to my Itching Scalp. Therefore, I am not Ready for his Second Coming.

T-[_] I have a BIG Tally Whacker, among other Big Things; and therefore, the Good Shepherd will Naturally Want me in his Holy Kingdom, which is a Good Government, which will not be Established on the Earth for at least another thousand Years: beCause it will Require at least a thousand Years for us to get ourselves Straightened Out, which is what an Erection Symbolizes. Yes, it is *Biblical,* which can be Proven in a Courtroom, if you can just Find some Lying Preacher to Interpret it that Way, who can Explain the Meanings of the Symbolical Things in the Tabernacle that Moses made, which had an Inner Court and an Outer Court, which had a Holy of Holies, wherein the Ark of the Covenant was Placed, along with the Ten Commandments Engraved on Stone Tablets, as well as the Bowl of Manna, and the Staff of Moses, which was no less than 7 feet Long, just to be a Shepherd's Staff, which had to be Broken into 2 Pieces, just to Fit it into the Ark: because it was only 3 feet Long, even though Jeremiah Revealed that a Cubit is the Length of a Man's Arm — that is, from the Tip of his Outstretched Fingers to his Armpit, which was and still is about 30 Inches. Therefore, if the Ark was 400 Cubits Long, it was about 1,000 feet long, which is HOW it Held 28,000+ Bovines, along with no less than a Million Bails of Hay for Feeding them, plus no less than 168,000,000 Gallons of Water, just for those Bovines, alone, not Counting the 3 Million Species of Birds and Insects that had to be Loaded into the Ark, which also had to be Fed and Watered in their Cages by only 8 People. Therefore, if you can Believe that Red Jew Fairy Tale, you can also Believe that my Tally Whacker is no less than 2 feet Long and 6 inches in Diameter when it is Stiff, which cannot be Fitted into any Hot Holes, even if it Wants to Fit in the Worst of Ways, and BEGS to be Satisfied! †§‡§§

U-[_] I am Utterly Amazed that a Righteous King would Write any such Provocative Words. Are you SURE that he is not an Impostor?

V-[_] You are a Victim of Superstitious Beliefs. Try Reading *Ezekiel 23,* which is Directly from the Mouth of Jehovah God!

W-[_] I Pray that I will Wither up and DIE, before I will let my Innocent Children read any such Evil Words, which are Pornographic.

X-[_] X-amount of People will Naturally Agree with you. However, if it is in the *Holy Bible,* it must be GOOD, even as the T Verse is also Good: beCause X-amount of People are Turned On by SEX; and without something Sexual to Read, they are not Satisfied, which is also WHY most of the Red Jew Movie Makers show some Naked Skin at the

Beginning of most of their Movies, which is called a "Lure," or "Temptation," which Lures Lustful People into Watching all such Movies, which is the Primary Reason for having "Joshua" in *The Ten Commandments* Movie with Charlton Heston, who was Born John Charles Carter, or Charlton John Carter, who was among the Best Actors who ever Lived; but, I Seriously Doubt that he will have any Position in the Kingdom of All that is GOOD: beCause no Liars are Welcome. (See *Revelation 21:8 and 22:15, KJV.* The word, *sorcerers,* should have been Translated as *Druggerers,* or People who Use and/or Sell Drugs. You can look it up in the Greek Dictionary in the Original *Strong's Exhaustive Concordance,* in the Big BOOK, which Reveals the Truth about it. Modern Commentators and Biblical Scholars like to Ignore all such Truths: because they have also Sold their Souls Down River, into Drug Slavery with Poor Nigger Jim.)

> Y-[_] I would Yield to God, and Pay my Tithes and Offerings Faithfully: beCause there are X-amount of People who are Born Blind, Deaf, Lame, or whatever, and would thus Need the Help of **"The New RIGHTEOUS One-World Government!"** Therefore, that is a GOOD Act to Love and Obey. However, if such a Government becomes Wicked, it is also Best to NOT Support it with any Tithes nor Offerings, whereby it will have to Straighten itself Out. ‡

> Z-[_] Even the Zebras Agree with you.

02-02 [_] No Businessman could Afford to Pay Swanky Wages: beCause of being far too Poor; but, **"The New RIGHTEOUS One-World Government"** could most certainly Afford it: beCause of having an Unlimited Amount of New Money to Work with. (See Verse 01.) Therefore, there would soon be a LOT of Money in Circulation with such a Good Government, whereby almost everyone would soon have Plenty of Money for Buying Foods, Clothing, Furniture, Computers, Telephones, or whatever, including Stone Dome Home Complexes, if they were Fools enough to do that, whereby they would only make Slaves of themselves for nothing. Indeed, it would be like the President Buying the White House, in Washington. What for? ‡

02-03 [_] All Communications and Transportations would be Provided by **"The New RIGHTEOUS One-World Government,"** along with Electricity, Water, Building Materials, Tools, Land, and whatever those **"Seven Great Armies of Working Soldiers"** might Need to Work with. Therefore, if X-amount of Watches are Needed, that Good Government will Provide Good Watches for everyone, and even Rolex Watches Studded with Diamonds: because we have an Abundance of Diamonds in this World of Wonders, and huge Warehouses full of them, which will now be Distributed to the Masses of People, Properly, who may Wear Diamond Rings, Bracelets, Watches, Necklaces and whatever.

> A-[_] I Agree — it would be Good to Open Up those Diamond Warehouses, and make Good Use of as many Diamonds as People might Want for Decorations. After all, there are likely enough Diamonds in this World of Wonders, whereby every Wombman in the World could have a Purse full of them!

> B-[_] I Believe it would be Unjust to Rob all of those Diamonds from those Warehouses, unless the Diamonds were given to the Slaves who Mined them Out, who could then Sell them for as much as they could get for them, which might be a Dollar for one of them. ‡

(The Equitable Wage System!)

C-[_] I Confess that such a Confiscation would be somewhat Just or Fair, if the Diamonds were Used Wisely for Decorating those **"Beautiful Swanky PALACES!"** Yes, God would no doubt Bless us for doing it, if we used the Diamonds for forming Special Words, which he has Inspired — such as Verse 02-01-L.

D-[_] That would not be Democratic; and therefore, that would be Unjust. Therefore, we must VOTE for what to Do with so many Diamonds.

E-[_] Educated and Enlightened People would just Naturally Vote for using those Diamonds in those **"Beautiful Swanky PALACES"** for the People who are most Worthy to Inherit them. After all, we cannot take anything with us when we Die. Therefore, we can only Enjoy such Good Things while we are Living. However, no one would Actually OWN such Diamonds, nor such Palaces: beCause they are far too Expensive; but, they would Look at them and Enjoy them for whatever it is Worth.

F-[_] I Fail to Understand WHY all such Diamonds are not now Sold on the Market, according to the DEMAND for them. After all, Capitalism is supposed to Work According to the SUPPLY and DEMAND. Therefore, a Diamond Ring should Cost about 10$: beCause of the Labor involved in making the Ring with a Machine. ‡

G-[_] God knows that it is not Right to Exploit those Lying Zionist Red Jews, who Own all of those Diamonds, who would Naturally be Jealous and Envious of us, if we Built those **"Beautiful Swanky PALACES!" (A New Concept in Living Habits — Palaces for Poor People!) By The Worldwide People's Revolution!® Book 066.**

H-[_] HUMBUG! Those Lying Zionist Red Jews can Kiss the Asses of Donkeys, if they do not Cheerfully Surrender ALL of their Diamonds, Rubies, Emeralds, Sapphires, Agates, and Gold to: **"The New RIGHTEOUS One-World Government!"** After all, **"The Swanky Associations of Working Soldiers"** is going to Built **"The Great World TEMPLE of PEACE"** for them, in Jerusalem, which will have some of the Finest Artwork in the World, as well as Plenty of Gold Cups, Platters, Bowls, and whatever they Want for Decorations in that Great Temple, which will have Polished Marble Walls, Polished Granite Floors, Carved Leather Swanky Easy Chairs, which lay back for Sleeping, as well as large Computer Screens, whereby a Million Visitors may Sit Back and RELAX, while they Listen to **"The Great Worldwide TELEVISED Court HEARING,"** which will no doubt Require Decades to Expose the Mountains of Outlandish Red Jew LIES that they have Written and Told, as if they were Truths! ‡

I-[_] I am an Innocent Child, who knows nothing about any such Red Jew Lies. Therefore, WHERE can I Learn about them on the Internet, whereby I might get myself Filled with HATRED for those Lying Red Jews, whereby I might Grow Up and become a TERRORIST, like George Warmonger Bush and Little Dick Chicanery? †§‡

J-[_] Justice Demands that all such Lying Snakes should Confess ALL of their Sins, or else be Boiled in HOT Used Motor Oil, after they are Proven Guilty, which they will be: beCause they are LIARS, and they also Know it for a Fact. Otherwise, they would be the

A List of FAIR Swanky Wages!

FIRST to Demand **"The Great Worldwide TELEVISED Court HEARING!"** And all of the Righteous People will say a Hearty, AMEN!

K-[_] King Jesus has Obviously already Returned, and is now Hiding Out somewhere in the Concrete Jungle: beCause no other Man ever Spoke such Powerful Words to us, as he Spoke, and is now Speaking. Therefore, let us Discover him, and Anoint him to be our Elected KING, before those Wicked Murderous Bloodthirsty Red Jews Kill him again! Indeed, nothing is beyond their Cruelties. After all, if he were a Bad Person, they could bring him to Court, and Try him for his Crimes. †§‡

L-[_] Lots of Laughs! King Jesus Died and went to Heaven, just like all of the other Good People since the Time of Adam and Eve. However, it does make a Good Story, and it also gives Hope to the Masses of People who Believe all such Jewish Fairy Tales; but, no Honest Educated Person would ever Believe those Lying Zionist Red Jews, who should all be Crucified with Radioactive Spent Rods from Nuclear Power Plants: beCause they are the Chief Proponents of all such Abominations! †§‡

M-[_] Dr. Martin Luther King, Junior, would Object to all such Cruelties, unless he Learned that it was that same Clan of Lying Zionist Red Jews who made SLAVES of the Africans, who were the Shipmasters, who saw it as another Money-mongering Capitalist Adventure, which filled up their Bank Accounts, which should Piss Off every Black Person in the World, who should DEMAND JUSTICE! †§‡

N-[_] NONSENSE! — those were Cruelties that took place 160 to 220 Years Ago! Therefore, there is no Way to get Justice for those Colored People who have Died so Long Ago, unless they have now been Born in Colored Families, in Africa — that is, IF that is WHERE God Wanted them to be Born Again, which he probably did for the Worst of them, who were found Guilty of Murders, or some Hate Crimes against other People and Animals, who have Mistreated Animals without any Justifiable Causes. Indeed, we are Supposed to Love our Naaberz as much as we Love ourselves, which would Naturally Include those Higher Forms of Animals — such as Horses, Cattles, Deers, Goats, Sheeps, Mules, Donkeys, Camels, Elephants, Dromedaries, Giraffes, Zebras, Burros, Reindeers, Caribous, Elks, Mooses, Yaks, Buffaloes, Bisons, Antelopes, Mountain Goats, Mountain Sheeps, and all such Lovable Creatures. Indeed, God made us Stewards over them, to Care for them, to Build Stone Dome Home Shelters for them, and Half-dome Stone Shelters, whereby they might Survive Extreme Temperatures, and also get something to Eat: so as to not Starve to Death. After all, what is more Innocent than a Fawn? ‡

O-[_] There is an Option. Indeed, whomever Wants to get Revenge on those Lying Thieving Zionist Jews should Check this Box [_] and the above Box with X's, whereby we can Hear their Complaints at: **"The Great Worldwide TELEVISED Court HEARING!"** After all, if someone has Hate in their Heart for someone, it must be with a Just Cause. Otherwise, they could Forgive them. †‡

P-[_] Some People are Professional Liars, who even make up False Stories about other People, just to get Sympathy or even Attention. Therefore, not all People can be Believed. However, if someone is Proven to be Lying about someone else at that Great Meeting of

(The Equitable Wage System!)

the Most Intelligent Minds, we will Kindly BOIL that Liar in HOT Used Motor Oil! Therefore, before you come to Court to Falsely Accuse anyone of anything, you must be Prepared to Suffer the Consequences: beCause those Consequences will be SEVERE! ‡

Q-[_] The Great Question is this, O Righteous King: **"Will anyone have anything Against anyone, after almost everyone has Moved into those "Beautiful Swanky PALACES!"?** And the Answer is, Probably NOT!

R-[_] I Maintain the Right to make my Complaints for the Mistreatments that I have Received from those Lying Red Jews, whereby they can Apologize to me and to whomever else that they have Offended. After all, that will not take any Skin Off of their Asses, nor Cause them to be Boiled in HOT Used Motor Oil. Therefore, they only need to Humble themselves and Confess the Provable Truths, whatever those Truths might be. ‡

S-[_] Saint Peter would Agree with you, and so do I.

T-[_] The Total Red Jew Lies might add up to an entire Set of Encyclopedias! Therefore, there is not enough TIME in anyone's Lifetime to Hear all such Lies, let alone give to those Lying Red Jews TIME to Argue with their Professional Lawyers. Therefore, I Suggest that we Round all of them up, like so many Cattle, and put them into NAZI Concentration Camps, if they do not Quickly Agree with Verse R, which is not Asking for very much from People who have Robbed other People of TRILLIONS of Dollars. Indeed, there are probably less than a half million of those Robbers, and only 10,000 or so Major Criminals among those, who can make Congressional Confessions, a thousand at a Time. ‡

U-[_] I Understand that certain Criminals cannot be brought to Court: because the Perpetrators of those Crimes have Long Ago DIED; but, that does not Mean that we cannot Hold Trials for their Crimes, and Expose all of them, if it will make anyone Feel Better, whereby they might Forgive such Criminals. ‡

V-[_] I am a Victim of the Jewish Holocaust, who would like to see all of those Nazis Boiled in HOT Used Motor Oil, if they do not Confess their Crimes Against us Honest White Jews. ‡

W-[_] World War 2 was a Zionist Red Jew Affair, you might say, who were also in Charge of those Concentration Camps, which you can Discover on the Internet. Just Search for: Benjamin Freedman, Eustace Mullins, David Irving, and Ernst Zundel, if you Want to Learn the Whole Truth about it. You should also Search for "HoloHOAX," which has some Good Videos on YouTube. However, if it can be Proven that those People are Lying, we can get the Record Straight, whereby everyone can be Happy. Yes, that is what **"The Great Worldwide TELEVISED Court HEARING"** is all about! ‡

X-[_] X-amount of People are just Naturally Forgetful when they get Old; and therefore, their Testimonies are Unreliable, even if they seem to be Sincere. Therefore, their Minds would have to be Refreshed by Means of FASTING, whereby they might get their Facts

25

more Correct. Moreover, whomever Fails to Check the above Box with an X is Suspect of being another Liar.

Y-[_] Yesterday came and Went. So, why do we not just Forget about those Evil Things that are Behind, and begin with a Clean Slate, as they say?

Z-[_] The Zeal of **The Worldwide People's Revolution!®** will make that Possible! Indeed, Wise People only have to Agree to Check the Appropriate Boxes, and we can Avoid all such Torments of Mind and Body, and go to Work for those Fair Swanky Wages!

02-04 [_] I find it most Interesting that our Elected King Imagines that almost all People in the World will Gladly Surrender their Lands and Mountains of Rocks to HIM, just beCause of being our Elected King, as if Greedy Selfish Red Jews would give up their Possessions, in Exchange for that UGLY Temple of Peace, which only a Small Fraction of the People in this World could get to Visit: beCause it would be Limited to only 2 Million Visitors per Day, divided into 7 Billion, equals about 3,500 Days, just to Accommodate all of them, which is about 10 Years — except that it will Require no less than one full Week, just to See all of the Museums and Stone Dome Homes within that Great Temple. However, the LOGISTICS will Present Massive Problems: beCause of Servicing all of those Millions of Visitors, who like to Eat, Drink, Piss, Shower and Sleep. Yes, there will be a Steady Steam of Traffic, coming and going, Swarming around like Bees at a Beehive! ‡

02-05 [_] Well, if People have Free Transportation, it is Possible that a Billion People will show up during one Week, unless everyone must have an Appointment, which would be Granted According to WHEN each Person Joined: **"The Swanky Associations of Working Soldiers,"** who would naturally have a Priority over anyone who Failed to Join it. Moreover, X-amount of People would not be Interested in Visiting that Temple, if they could Visit those **"GLORIOUS Swanky Hotels Castles and Fortresses,"** which will have **"Beautiful Swanky PALACES!"** Indeed, most Swanky Fortresses will be far more Architecturally Beautiful than **"The Great World TEMPLE of PEACE"**: beCause of those Palaces, and beCause of the Spectacular 3-dimentional Views, which will not be Possible at the Tempe: because it must be most Visible from the Surrounding Swanky Hotels for Visitors: beCause there will be no nearby Swanky Fortresses, just to be Able to House those Visitors in the Hotels, by Advanced Reservations. ‡

02-06 [_] So, O Elected King, is it Fair to say that Jerusalem will be the Most Crowded Place on the Earth?

02-07 [_] Well, I have no Idea what the Future will bring with it; but, my Educated Guess is that it will be very Crowded: beCause of those Fascinating Trials in the Temple, which will Cover a Great Range of Important Subjects, including Fake Moon Landings, UFO's, Aliens, Angels, Ghosts, Resurrections, Environmental Problems, Criminal Minds, Crazy People, Curious Animals, Special Plants, Special People, Arts, Gymnastics, Ballets, Concerts, Special Speeches, Special Sermons, Special Books, Poems, Songs, and whatever People can come up with. Trust me, it will be a First Class Entertainment Center for the World, without a Boring Minute to Waste.

(The Equitable Wage System!)

02-08 [_] So, O Elected King, will you be giving Special Speeches in that Great Temple?

02-09 [_] Well, that will Depend on whether or not I am still Alive, or how I Feel at the Time, and how Long it Requires to get that Temple Finished. I would say that its Construction would Require about 6 Years, once the Blueprints are made up, which Architects and Engineers should now be Working on, just to Save Time, after Studying all of my Inspired Books, which have Bits of Information here and there throughout those Books: beCause that is the Way that God Inspired them, even as this Book has no Direct Connection with that Subject; but, it does have an Indirect Connection, which will be Understandable, later on.

02-10 [_] So, O King of the Mountain, will Famous Authors of Books and Magazine Articles be Invited to Speak or Read in **"The Great World TEMPLE of PEACE!"**?

02-11 [_] Well, that all Depends on what Information they might have to Share with us, which will have to be Judged by the Elected Officials.

02-12 [_] So, O King, what about the Voices and Opinions of the Dissenters — will they not be Heard?

02-13 [_] Well, I would say that at least one Hour per Day should be Dedicated to Hearing those Voices. However, just to make it Fair, everyone will be Welcome to Address their Honest Opinions to: **"FREEDUM uv SPEECH!" (U Speshoul Maguzeen uv Onust Upinyunz!) By The Worldwide People's Revolution!®** Book 030-0001—9999. In other Words, no one will be Blocked Out. Furthermore, each Opinion will be Graded for its Value within those Magazines: so as to not Waste People's Precious Time reading Ridiculous Opinions nor Religious Nonsense.

02-14 [_] O you Silly King, if anything on the Earth has been a Waste of Precious Time, it has been Reading this Insane Book, which has barely Mentioned Wages, nor the Injustices of Capitalism, which is an Evil Economic System that takes Advantage of the Lower Classes, who used to be Slaves and Servants, who Lived in little Shacks and Shanties, who had a Lifespan of less than 40 Years, who often Died from Horrible Diseases for a Lack of Medical Treatments, who Died by the Multiple Millions in Poor Nations, like China and India, who often just Rotted on the Streets, or were Eaten by Dogs and Vultures: because no one Cared for them. Therefore, we have come a long ways Forward since those Days; but, now it seems that America is going Backwards, and no longer Holds World Records for a High Standard of Living, like it used to. ‡

02-15 [_] Well, my Friend, you just have to be Patient with this Book: because I will Try to Cover all of the Bases, as they say, and Address any Important Subjects that concern Wages and the Injustices of Capitalism, Communism, Socialism, Fascism, and whatever — all of which are False Economic Systems, which have Produced the Pollution, Crimes, Taxes, Sicknesses, Diseases, Divorces, Broken Hearts, and all of the Troubles that we have nowadays, which never Needed to be, except that Humanity has certain Lessons to be Learned, which is WHY God has Allowed it to Happen, which has Inspired some People to say that "God does not Exist!" Indeed, it is easy to Understand WHY those People come up with such "Rational" Conclusions: beCause the *Bible, Koran, The Book of Mormon,* and other Religious Books make it out that God was and still is Dealing in the Affairs of Men all along; and, if not Collectively, at least Personally, whereby some People seem to have a Close Relationship with their God, and even Sincerely

27

Believe that he "Talks" with them. However, when you Inquire concerning just Exactly HOW or WHAT their God "said" to them, they are generally Dumbfounded, and often Confess that they just Imagined that they Heard some Inner Voice, which did not Actually Speak to them. Furthermore, if you Prodded them for any Solutions that God might have Revealed to them, which would Prove to be Workable, and Reasonable, you might Discover that they are even more Blank-minded: beCause, like most Politicians, Preachers, Doctors, Lawyers, and Professors, they have ZERO Solutions that are Acceptable by Sane People, whereas my Solutions are Acceptable by ALL Sane People, and can easily be Proven to be Practical, Reasonable, and Workable. After all, I am not Proposing the Construction of Swanky Fortresses on MARS, nor on the Moon; but, only on this Good Earth, whereby our Basic and Major Problems can be Solved, and without going to WAR! Indeed, even Warmongers must Confess that my Plan is Far Superior to all others. †§‡

— Chapter 03 —

What is Wrong with the Welfare State?

03-01 [_] When People Depart from the Land that can Feed and Clothe them, they are Automatically at the Mercy of the Welfare State, if they should not Find Employment, and right away. Indeed, they Immediately Sacrifice their Freedoms on the Land, for the Slavery that is Offered to them within Cities of Confusion. First of all, like Slaves, they must go Knocking on the Doors of Businessmen and Businesswomen, BEGGING for some Work to do, in Exchange for whatever Wages are Offered to them, which can easily be Minimum Wages, if there is a Long Line of Potential Employees: beCause the Big Boss can say, "I have lots of Slaves to Choose from, and therefore all of them are Expendable. In Fact, if I do not Happen to Like the Looks of any of them, I can Fire them, and Pick New Employees from among this Crowd of Ignorant Beggars." And thus is his Reasoning, which none of the Slaves nor Beggars can Argue Against: beCause they are Desperate for WORK, just to Earn some Money, in Order to be Able to EAT and Drink. Therefore, if they cannot Find a Job, they are at the Mercy of the Welfare State, which Offers to them Food Stamps and Welfare Checks, which never Cover all of the Costs; but, it Helps them to Survive, which is a Daily Struggle for a Family, and Especially if it is a one-parent "Family," as in one Mother with 3 Children, which is often the Case in **"The Divided States of United Lies!"**

03-02 [_] O Elected King, if a Person is not Born into a Prosperous Family, whereby he or she has the Great Advantage of Financial Support, whereby he or she can Obtain a College Education, he or she is at the Mercy of the Welfare State, which, itself, is at the Mercy of the Tax Slaves, who can never seem to Pay Enough Taxes to Cover all of the Costs of the Welfare State. Indeed, that is a Typical European Problem, in Greece, for Example, which is not a Major Exporter of Capitalist Products, as is Germany, which has always been a Major Producer of Exported Goods: beCause they are very Industrious People, by Nature, while the Italians are only Moderately Industrious, and the Greeks would rather have Drinking Parties, and Enjoy a Relaxed

(The Equitable Wage System!)

Lifestyle without any Stress: because they have a *Garden of Eden* Mentality, you might say, even as most People in the World have, who would much rather Live a Relaxed Lifestyle, even as you have Proposed for almost all People in the World, who could be Living in Peace within those **"GLORIOUS Swanky Hotels Castles and Fortresses!" (Beautiful Planned City States for WISE Intelligent Well-Educated People with Common Sense and Good Understanding!) By The Worldwide People's Revolution!®** Book 019. Indeed, that is Physically Possible, and most Practical: beCause People were not Designed to Live with such Stress as Modern Societies try to Live with, whereby they are Under Constant PRESSURE to do everything Perfectly and Precisely, as if they were making Rolex Watches, which must be Flawless! Indeed, just Try to Imagine HOW a Poor Mexican Fruit Picker, or Goat Herder, for Example, could Manage to Handle such a Job as making Rolex Watches! It is simply NOT in his Bloodline to Do such Work. However, it is Highly Possible for such a Person to Attend to his own Garden, once he is Taught HOW to do it, whereby he can Relax, and take his Sweet Time to do it as he Wants to, and to Ask some Master Gardener to Help him, if he has some Problem. After all, most Mexicans make Good Servants; but, not Good Masters: beCause they do not have a Sense of Perfection. Indeed, if you gave to them all of the Professional Tools and Building Materials to Work with, they could never Build anything so Precise as a German, Italian, Englishman, Russian, Spaniard, Swede, Norwegian, Swiss, Dane, or Frenchman might do: beCause those Mexicans have too much Indian Blood in them, which is True for most Africans, who Lack a Sense of Perfection that is among Europeans, Asians, and Egyptians. †§‡

03-03 [_] Well, I have been saying for 30+ Years that X-amount of People were Born to be Masters, and X-amount were Born to be Servants. {See www.Amazon.com for: **"A Sound Argument for Masters and Servants!" (WHY Everyone Needs a Good Master, and every Master Needs Good Obedient Servants!) By The Worldwide People's Revolution!®** Book 008.} Yes, it can easily be Proven in a Courtroom that People have Different Skills and Abilities, which is Obvious by their WORKS. Indeed, practically all of the Artistic Buildings in the World were Built Long Ago, when People's Minds were Working Better, which we would have a Difficult Time Duplicating, Today — such as the Pantheon and Saint Peter's Basilica in Rome, which is about 20 Times as large as the Shrine of Immaculate Conceptions in Washington, D.C. However, that is not to say that the Shine is not Worth your Time to Visit it: beCause it will give to you some Idea how MAGNIFICENT Saint Peter's Basilica is, which would likely Cost a Trillion Dollars, Today — except that no Michelangelo is around to Manage the Construction of it. Nevertheless, when Compared with **"The Great World TEMPLE of PEACE,"** that Basilica will be among the Lower Class Construction Projects: beCause that Great Temple will be a thousand Times as Big and Beautiful! †§‡

03-04 [_] O Elected King, what if some Mentally-ill Lunatic Crashes a Jet Airliner into that Great Temple, in Jerusalem: beCause of having some Islamic Belief that IDOLS are EVIL — HOW will we Prevent that from Happening?

03-05 [_] Well, the most Simple Prevention is to do Away with all such Airplanes, Guided Missiles, Bombs, and whatever might be used by Fools to Destroy such Artistic Buildings, which do not Need any Idols in them. Indeed, in that Case, we can all Compromise with the Muslims, and not make any Idols for **"The Great World TEMPLE of PEACE,"** in Jerusalem: beCause those Idols are not Needed, much less Wanted. After all, there is no *Biblical Law* against Polished Marbles, Granites, Onyxes, Agates, Gemstones, Silver, Gold, nor any such Things, which can be made very Artistic without making Images of People, Animals, Flowers, Trees, nor any such Things — even though the Instructions to Moses clearly Command the Israelites to make such Images for the Tabernacle, and Pomegranates for the Garments, and even for the Temple. {See *Exodus 28:33; 39:24—25; First Kings 7:18, 20, 42; Second Kings 25:17* (notice that the Pillar was 45 feet high!), *Second Chronicles 3:16; 4:13;* and *Jeremiah 52:22—23.*}

03-06 [_] O King, are you Suggesting that the Lincoln Memorial in the District of Colombian Drug Addicts, is an IDOL, just beCause it is an Image of Abraham Lincoln?

03-07 [_] Well, the very *Second Commandment* clearly states: *"You shall not make unto you any Graven Image of any Living Thing, nor any Picture or Painting of the Likeness of any Thing that is in the Sky above you, nor that is on the Land about you, nor that is in the Water below the Land, in the Rivers and Seas; and neither shall you Bow Down yourselves to any such Things, nor Serve them as Rulers over you: because I, the Great Creator, your Supreme Ruler am a Jealous God, who is Rewarding the Iniquities of the Fathers on the Children, even unto the Third and Fourth Generations of those Ignorant Fools who Hate me without any Justified Causes, as if I were the Unholy One who Created all of those Evil Mosquitoes, Ticks, Fleas, Lice, Weevils, Poisonous Spiders, Scorpions, Snakes, Bears, Lions, Wolves, Jackals, Hyenas, Foxes, Coyotes, Dogs, Hogs, and all such Unclean Creatures, not to Mention a million Viruses, Sicknesses, Diseases, Accidents, and all such Evil Things, which are Inventions of Satan, the Devil, who Imported many of those Evil Creatures into this World from other Worlds: because he is a Mischievous Character, and a Great Deceiver, who would have you to Believe that it is Good to Worship Idols, and to make Images of Various Kinds of Stone, Brass, Gold, Silver, Wood, Clay, and whatever, as if those Vain Things could make you Healthy and Happy. Therefore, Listen to me, O you Ignorant Fools, and I will Teach to you a few Important Truths, whereby you can Live in Perfectly Good Health, and be most Happy. Indeed, the Devil would have everyone to be Sick and Miserable; but, I would have everyone to be Healthy, Wealthy, and WISE. Therefore, Strain yourselves to Listen Intently to me. Yes, Dig the Wax of Unbelief OUT of your Spiritual Ears, and Listen Intently with both of your Outer Ears and your Inner Ears.*

03-08 [_] *"First of all, you must not Practice the Vain Customs of the Heathen People all around you: beCause they are Extremely Ignorant, who Suffer with Various Kinds of Sicknesses and Diseases: beCause of Ignoring the Dietary Laws, which I gave to Adam, who was the First White Man that I Created in this World, who had a Perfect Body, being Created in my own Image: beCause each World Needs someone to Govern it, and that someone Needs a Family to Help him to Govern it: beCause it is far too Big for just one Person to Properly Manage it, which is WHY People Need to be WISE, and Establish a Righteous One-World Government, which has a Righteous King in Charge of it, who Helps those Wise People to Build Beautiful Planned City States, whereby each City State can Govern itself According to its own Elected Laws and Flexible Rules: beCause not all Peoples are just Alike. In Fact, no one was Created Equal with anyone else: beCause each Person is Unique and Special, being Born for a Special Reason, being like Different Parts of a Great Body, which must Work Together in Harmony, in Order to make it Possible for the Body of that Good Government to Function Correctly, whereby all Parts of the Body can be Healthy and Happy, According to their own Wisdom, whereby each City State is Free to Choose whatever they Want, and to Live with other People of Like-mindedness, who can easily be Discovered by each Person Filling Out and Filing the Complete SURVEYS of their VALUES, whereby the Good Honest People can be SEPARATED from the Evil Dishonest*

(The Equitable Wage System!)

People: beCause it is not Justice for Righteous People to Support Wicked People; but, Righteous People should Support Righteous People, even as the Liver Supports the Heart, and the Heart Supports the Head, and the Head Supports the entire Body of a Good Government.

*03-09 [ ] "Therefore, in Order to have Harmony among all of the Nations, there must be a Righteous One-World GovernMINT, which simply Mints and Prints the Necessary Brand New Money with New Symbols and Numbers, in Order to Use that Money WISELY, in Order to HIRE whomever is Willing and Able to Learn and Work, according to a List of FAIR Swanky Wages, whereby he who does the Most Work is Paid the Most, and she who does the Least Work is Paid the Least: beCause that is Justice for them. Indeed, all of the Young Men should be Happy to Join Seven Great Armies of Working Soldiers, which are Furnished with the Correct Tools for Moving Mountains of Rocks, Sand, Topsoil, and whatever is Needed for Building Beautiful Planned City States for ALL of the People who WANT them, and that Stonework will Represent that New Money, which must be Earned by Honest Labor, without the Use of any Bankers, without any Loans, without any Usury, and without any Taxes, which are Collected beCause of Heathen Customs, which you must not Practice: beCause those Customs Produce X-amount of Criminals, whom you do not Want nor Need. In Fact, if you Discover some Potential Criminal within your Beautiful Planned City State, who is not Willing to Learn, Believe, Love, nor Obey all of my Commandments, you can simply Cast Out that Person, and have nothing more to do with him or her: beCause he or she can go Knock on the Door of a Lost Creature's Hotel, if he or she gets Hungry, whereby he or she can Attend Classes about HOW to Live Properly: so as to not be a Problem for the Societies that are around him or her. Indeed, that Good One-World Government must have ONE Kind of Money, only, which has the Exact same Value in all of the Nations, whereby it can be Used Wisely for Buying Goods and Services; but, NOT Good Instructions: beCause all Good Instructions will be Provided, Free of any Charges, by **"The New RIGHTEOUS One-World Government!"** Yes, that Good Government must have certain Duties and Performances, including Provisions for Communications and Transportations, which must be FREE of any Charges, being Provided by **"The Swanky Associations of Working Soldiers,"** which is made up of VOLUNTEERS, only: beCause no one should be Forced to do Good Works: beCause that is Satan's Way of Doing Things, not mine. Therefore, if you have to Force someone to Do something, it is Obviously Wrong. However, that is also a Flexible Rule: beCause there are certain Times when People should be Forced to Answer Questions, or else be Whipped for it: beCause anyone can say, 'I am Sorry, but I do not know the Answer to your Question.' Or, 'Please Repeat the Question in such a Way that I might be Able to Understand it: beCause I am a Grade School Dropout.' Otherwise, People will be getting by with Murder, Stealing, Lying, Cheating, Bribing, Counterfeiting Money, Raping, Sodomizing, Committing Adultery, and all Kinds of Evils, which will be a Great Disgrace to a Righteous Government, and a Great Shame on all of the People, who would rather have Peace, Cooperation, and Harmony.*

*03-10 [ ] "Now, you might be Wondering just HOW such a Good Government could Obtain all of the Land, Silver, Gold, Mountains of Rocks, Sand, Gravel, Rivers of Water, and everything that is Needed for Producing those **"GLORIOUS Swanky Hotels Castles and Fortresses,"** whereby the Masses of People might Prosper with True Prosperity, even while Living in **"Beautiful Swanky PALACES,"** which none of them could ever Afford to Buy? Well, the most Simple Solution is for those Masses of People to DEMAND **"The Great Worldwide TELEVISED Court HEARING!" (That Great Meeting of the Most Intelligent Minds!) By The Worldwide People's Revolution!®** Book 041. Yes, those Masses of People must first of all Learn* *about this Plan for Worldwide Peace and True Prosperity, which will be a simple matter of Publishing this one Inspired Book, which can be put into every Mailbox in the United States of America, first of all: beCause they have the Best Opportunity for bringing it all about, which they may Accept or Reject, which will be their Decisions to make. After all, I will not Suffer for their Unbelief nor Disobedience; but, they will most Certainly Suffer for it: beCause those Fortresses will not get Built without the United Effort of* **"Seven Great Armies of Working Soldiers,"** *who should also be Volunteers. However, if there are not Enough Volunteers to get the Work Done, it is not a Sin to DRAFT Young Working Soldiers, just as long as they are Paid HALF as much Pay for their Services, as a Just Reward for their Non-cooperation. After all, they are Welcome to Change their Minds at any Time, and thus Volunteer to Join* **"The Swanky Associations of Working Soldiers,"** *who will Specialize in certain Crafts, or otherwise just Do whatever they are Asked to Do, according to the Demands for such Work. For Example, if there are a LOT of Apples to be Harvested, most of those Voluntary Working Soldiers will do the Picking and Gathering and Processing, or whatever is Needed: beCause, in Exchange for their Cheerful Services, they will Inherit those* **"Beautiful Swanky PALACES!"** *Yes, they will get to Live in them until they Die, without Paying any Rent, without Buying any Insurance, without being Taxed, and without Owning anything other than their Personal Possessions — such as their Combs, Toothbrushes, Fingernail Trimmers, Spoons, Ink Pens, Papers, Books, Computers, Musical Instruments, Fine Hand-crafted Furniture, and whatever Movable Items that they might Want to Own: beCause ALL of the Buildings, Highways, Bridges, Tunnels, Moats, Subway Trains, Electric Wires, Elevators, Escalators, Swimming Pools, Gymnasiums, Theaters, Auditoriums, Ball Parks, Bowling Alleys, Skating Rinks, Tennis Courts, Greenhouses, Fruit Tree Houses, Cisterns, Water Pumps, Pipes, and all such Things will Belong to* **"The New RIGHTEOUS One-World Government,"** *which will Mint and Print the Necessary Brand New Money for Hiring those Voluntary Working Soldiers to Build all such Things, and the Stonework will Represent that New Money, which will be the Best Money in all of the World: beCause it will have to be Earned by Honest Labor, without any Loans, without any Interest, and without any Taxes: beCause all of those Voluntary Working Soldiers will Gladly Pay a Voluntary TITHE of 10% of their Income for the Support of their Good Government Officials, including Doctors, Lawyers, Judges, Professors, Teachers, Preachers, Priests, Scientists, Chemists, Inventors, and the Elite Class of Professional People, who will also get to Live in those* **"Beautiful Swanky PALACES,"** *in Exchange for their Services, while being Paid According to their Labors. For Example, an Elected King may Receive 40 Dollars per Hour for his Services, plus 10$ per Hour for the Stress of his Responsibilities; or, a Total of 50$ per Hour, while a House Cleaner may Receive 50$ per Hour, and a Professional Cook may Receive 60$ per Hour, plus 10$ for Stress; and a Tile Setter may Receive the same Pay, plus 10$ for his Stress. Likewise, a Person who Hoes Weeds in a Hot Sweaty Garden may Receive 50$ per Hour, plus 10$ for the Stress of the Heat or Cold, which 10$ should be used to Cover his Insurance for his Health Care, if he does not Choose to Live with other People who Choose to Follow Strict Dietary Laws, whereby they will not Need any Health Care, who may use their Stress Pay as they Wish, once they Retire, after just 6 Years of Labor: because, within only 6 Years of Labor, all of those Swanky Hotels and Fortresses will be Finished, if you Follow the Instructions of my Selected King, who is the Inspired Author of my Good Books, including this Book. Therefore, let no one Mock him for his Weaknesses: beCause everyone has his or her Weaknesses, which can easily be Proven in a Courtroom.*

(The Equitable Wage System!)

03-11 [_] *"However, if anyone Imagines that he or she is now Perfect, and has no Need of any Improvements, let him or her Step Forward at **"The Great Worldwide TELEVISED Court HEARING,"** and Demonstrate to us just HOW to be Perfect, after being put in Charge of the Court! Yes, if such a Person Claims to have Better Solutions than my Selected King, let him or her Present those Solutions, or else Keep Silent: beCause it is not Wise to make a Fool of yourself for nothing. After all, it is now Possible and most Practical for People to Communicate their Ideas by Means of the Internet, by E-mail Letters, which everyone can Study. Yes, they should Send their Honest Opinions to **"The New RIGHTEOUS One-World Government,"** which will Post those Opinions in: **"FREEDUM uv SPEECH!" (U Speshoul Maguzeen uv Onust Upinyunz!)**, whereby their Opinions can be Studied and Responded to by whomever is Wise, whereby the Best Solutions can easily be Discovered, and put into Inspired Books by my Selected King, who already has the Best Solutions that I can Think of, and I am the Creator of this World. Therefore, if I cannot Think of Better Solutions, how can you? Nevertheless, there is the Possibility of it: beCause of Communicating with some Higher God. After all, the Gods like to Play Intellectual Games, you might say: beCause they Enjoy it, and so do People, who are Created in the Images of those Gods. Therefore, it is just a Natural Thing for People of Greater Intellect to Tease those of Lesser Intellects, which may be Fun; but, I can Assure you that my Selected King is not Playing any Silly Intellectual Games with you, except to Tease the so-called 'Intellectuals,' who would Naturally say that I should get my Single Quotes and Double Quotes straightened out in this Speech. However, it is just another Flexible Rule to Follow, which is Harmless, with or without Single or Double Quotation Marks: beCause it is Understood that none of these Words are Actually Quotations from anyone, and Certainly NOT from the Most High God, who has Better Things to Attend to. Nevertheless, the Design is Perfect for Mockingbirds and Ignorant Fools, who also Mock the Capitalized Words, the Long Sentences, the Rambling Thoughts, the Irrelevant Subjects, the Strange Ideas, and even Falsely Claim that God is DEAD, as if the Holy Spirit DIED, when she is an Immortal Spirit, who can Speak to the Mind of whomever is Listening with their Spiritual Ears Wide Open, even as my Selected King has done during many Occasions, whose Inspired Words of Provable Truths can be found in hundreds of Good Books, which should be Carefully Studied by all Wise People: beCause it is a Way to Collect Wisdom in your Heads, whereby you might make Good Judgments: beCause of having Good Understanding, which is one of the Greatest of the Gifts of the Gods.*

03-12 [_] *"Now, I Fully Realize that you People have many Questions to Ask, which have already mostly been Answered within the Inspired Books of my Selected King, whom you must now Adopt as your Selected King, until at Last he can be Elected by the Masses of People, Worldwide, after they Learn all of the Wonderful Things that will be Presented at:* **"The Great Worldwide TELEVISED Court HEARING!"** *Yes, you have no Idea what Information will be Presented, until you DEMAND that Great Meeting of the Most Intelligent Minds! Indeed, I have Inspired many People in all Nations to Record their Provable Truths, which can be and should be and must be Collected into* **"The Swanky Truth-brary,"** *whereby Future Generations of Wise People might Study all such Inspired Books, if they can Discover the Time to do so, which they will Discover after their* **"Beautiful Swanky PALACES,"** *have been Completed. Yes, you must go about it like going to War, whereby all Efforts are put forth to Accomplish it as Quickly and as Efficiently as Possible, BEFORE the Icebergs MELT, and the Oceans RISE by 40 feet or more. Yes, you must Plan those* **"GLORIOUS Swanky Hotels Castles and Fortresses"** *for such Rising Tides, which will be Difficult to do around Coastal Areas: beCause Underground Railways would be Filling Up with Water. Therefore, it is Wise to put those Railways Above the*

33

Rising Tide Levels, and even Forsake most of the Coastal Cities, including New York City, Washington, D.C., Los Angeles, Miami, Houston, Seattle, Boston, London, Hong Kong, Moscow, Hamburg, Sydney, Naples, Rio de Janeiro, and any City near Sea Level: beCause they are likely to be Drowned Out, unless you STOP Polluting the Atmosphere with your Abominations, Worldwide. Indeed, you should Immediately Funnel your Time, Money, Materials, and Energy into the Construction of those **"GLORIOUS Swanky Hotels Castles and Fortresses,"** *beginning with the Hotels, which can be used by the Voluntary Working Soldiers, until the Fortresses are Built, which must be Built for all of the People who Want to Live within them, after which the Castles can be Built, after all of the People have been Secured within their Swanky Fortresses. Meanwhile, you can be Gathering Up and Destroying those Abominations that I HATE, including those Stinking Noisy Motorcycles, Motor Scooters, Lawnmowers, Cars, Bombs, and Vain Things that you do not Need for True Prosperity. Yes, you must Transition your Way from the Great False Economy into the New and Wonderful Economy of* **"The New RIGHTEOUS One-World Government,"** *whereby nearly every Person on this Earth will become Moderately RICH, without Telling any Lies, nor Selling any Trash! Yes, all Tools should be made of First Class Quality, so as to Endure the Test of Time — that is, IF they are Necessary Tools, such as Shears for Mowing Off Grasses and Weeds around Fruit Trees, until those Fruit Trees are Grown Up enough to make it Practical to keep Sheeps Grazing around the Trees, who will keep the Grasses and Weeds under Control. Otherwise, you may use Swanky Mulching Rocks, which are Slabs of Granite or Hard Limestone that have been Cut Perfectly 2 feet square and 1-inch thick, which have one inch Cut Off of each Corner: so that when they are Fitted Together on Level Ground, they form Perfect Places for Planting Grape Vines, Berry Bushes, Watermelons, Cantaloupes, Squashes, Tomatoes, Cucumbers, Bell Peppers, Broccoli, Cauliflower, Cabbages, Pole Beans, English Peas, and whatever you Choose to Plant and Eat, which Mulching Rocks will also Protect the Ground from Sunlight, and Provide a Better Home for Earthworms, while Keeping much of the Moisture in the Ground, which will Save much Water and much Time doing the Weeding, according to:* **"The LUSCIOUS All-Mineral Organic Method of Gardening!" (HOW to Grow DELICIOUS Satisfying Foods for Potential Kingz and Kweenz in Swanky PALACES!) By The Worldwide People's Revolution!®,** *Book 021, which will Require a LOT of Work to get everything Set Up Properly; but, once you get it Set Up Properly, your Gardening will become a Sheer JOY! Therefore, have Faith in what I have Taught to you, and get my Selected King Elected to Govern you before you Fools Destroy yourselves!"*

03-13 [_] O Elected King, why did you Stop? I could Listen to such Sermons all Day Long, and never get Bored with them.

03-14 [_] Well, maybe you could, and I certainly could; but, some People might be Offended with so many Provable Truths. Besides that, it is not Necessary that God should have to Explain all such Things to us. Therefore, let us See what Happens with his Inspired Words of Provable Truths. Indeed, you are Welcome to make Copies of Chapter 03, and pass them out for Free on the Streets, just to See what Happens with all such Words. After all, they are bound to be Accepted and Rejected, which will form an Opposition, whereby we may Divide and Conquer! Yes, it will be THEM Against US, if they Reject the Provable Truths within this Chapter. However, in Order to PREVENT all such Divisions, whereby everyone is in Agreement, it is Best if all People Carefully Read the entire Book, whereby almost everyone will Agree to Establish **"The New RIGHTEOUS One-World Government,"** which will have to Begin with: **"The Great Worldwide TELEVISED Court HEARING!"** Yes, it always goes right back around to that Conclusion, no matter how you Think about it: beCause the ONE and ONLY Way that we can Solve our Massive Problems is to Build those **"GLORIOUS Swanky Hotels Castles and Fortresses!"**

03-15 [_] I Beg your Pardon, O Silly King: beCause there is a Better Way to Solve our Massive Problems, which is for everyone to Repent of all of their Sins, and Believe in the Teachings of Jesus Christ, who said to not Accept any Thoughts for Tomorrow, for what we might Eat, Drink, Wear, nor even where to Live: beCause the Evils of each Day are Sufficient, without Adding any Evils to it by Thinking about Planting Gardens, Vineyards, and Orchards, much less Building Billions of Cisterns for Water Storage, and Building **"Beautiful Swanky PALACES,"** which we do not Need to be Healthy nor Happy: beCause it is Possible to be Happy if you are just Positive-minded, and do not Think about Providing yourself with Tools, Gardens, Houses, Workshops, Sales Shops, nor any other Vain Things. Yes, you may now Relax, and just Sit under a Juniper Tree with Jonah, and HOPE that some Holy Angels have Mercy on you by Means of the Welfare State: beCause Gabriel is in Charge of it! †§‡§§

— Chapter 04 —

More Nails in the Boards!

04-01 [_] Now, the Capitalist Plan for getting Prepared for Tornadoes, is to put more Nails in the Boards in the Wooden / Plastic Firetrap Mouse-infested Cockroach Den, which only Slightly Improve on it: beCause no Respectable Tornado is very Concerned with any such Nails, since it is quite Possible to LIFT UP and Remove the entire House, if not Rip it into Shreds! After all, entire Forests have been Transformed into Proverbial "Toothpicks," lying all about, which some People have called "the Wrath of God," even though it is the Natural Wrath of Nature, which knows nothing about any God: beCause the Wind does not have a Mind, whereby it might Think and Remember anything, which is also True of Water and Fire, which are Equally as Destructive and Violent in their own Ways. ‡

04-02 [_] However, there is one Thing that all Fires have to Respect, and that is the Durability of ROCKS, which are not much Bothered by Forest Fires, which Burn rather Cool, when Compared with Volcanoes and Molten Lava, which comes out of the Bowels of the Earth, which is a Strange Creature, itself, you might say, which Scientists are only Beginning to Understand a Fraction of: beCause of the Complications of the Earth, which has barely been Penetrated by Mankind. The Inner Workings are still a Mystery, and there are many Theories about just Exactly what might be going on down there in the Bowels of the Earth; but, for Sure, there is no Doubt about what is going on all about the Surface of the Earth, which has been Studied for thousands of Years by all Kinds of People. It is Fair to say that a Swanky Fortress can be Built in such a Way that a Forest Fire could not have any Great Effects on it: beCause of Building Stone Walls, Moats, and Hayfields all around it. Therefore, even if the Hayfield should Burn, it would have very little Effect on the Stone Walls, and no Effects on the Moats, whereas the Normal

American House has little or no Protection from Raging Fires, which is Proven in California every Year, and ever since they began to Build such Houses over there, in about 1840.

04-03 [_] So, O Elected King, if the Elected Politicians had any Love for our Souls, they would make those Bankers Change their Ways, and only Loan Money for Building GOOD Stone Houses with Concrete Roofs, huh? Would that not Solve the House-fire Problem, and the Tornado and Termite Problems?

04-04 [_] Well, it would be a Great Improvement; but, it would not Solve the Heating nor Cooling Bill Problem: beCause those Rocks can get Cold, as well as Hot. However, if the Solid Stone Walls are 10 feet or more THICK, they form what is called a "Heat Bank," or "Cold Bank," which can be used for Heating or Cooling the House, which is the Principle that is Employed in the Construction of Saint Peter's Basilica, which has Double Stone Walls, each of which are 4 feet thick, with a 4-feet-wide Walkway between those 2 Walls, whereby Windows can be Opened or Closed, which is an Optional Plan for Heating and Cooling, which just Happens to Work Well in Rome: beCause of not getting Extremely Cold nor Extremely Hot, as it does in **"The Divided States of United Lies,"** which goes to Extremes, whereby it might get down to minus 30 °F in Montana or North Dakota, or as much as 110 °F in August. Therefore, with such Radical Changes in the Weather, it calls for THICK Stone Walls, which are 10 to 20 feet thick, which can be made by placing Fill Dirt between Solid Stone Walls, which are used for Heat Banks. After all, no Amount of Cold Weather can Work its way through such a Thick Wall, which must also Cover the Roof. Therefore, a Swanky Stone DOME HOME is the Ideal Way to Build such a Good House, whereby one Dome is Connected to another Dome by Stone Barrel-vaults, even as I have already Explained in several other Books, whereby such a House is Mouse-proof, Termite-proof, Hail-proof, Tornado-proof, Fireproof, Insurance-proof, and Self-air-conditioned, which easily Pays for the House within one Person's Lifetime, if it is not too BIG. However, I do not like to Live in a Tiny "Cave House," you might say, and neither would any other Sane Person, and especially when you Consider the Fact that there is LOTS of Space for all such Stone Dome Home Complexes, which should all have Gardens on their Roofs, which is made Possible and Practical by having the City Built in TERRACES, whereby everyone's Garden is directly in Front of his or her House, and NOT on the Roof, whereby such a Person would have to go Up and Down Stairways when he or she is 290 Years Old, which could Prove to be Burdensome with Baskets of Groceries. ‡

04-05 [_] O Elected King, it does seem like you have it all Figured Out, except for HOW to get yourself in Control of this World of Woes, whereby you might Invite those Voluntary Working Soldiers to go to WORK for those Good Swanky Wages, whereby a Person might Collect enough Money during just one Week to Live Well for a Month! Indeed, you might get them to Work for only one Day per Week: beCause of Paying to them too many Wages, or too High Wages, or too much Wages — I have no Idea HOW to say it Correctly. ‡

04-06 [_] Well, before anyone can Join **"The Swanky Associations of Working Soldiers,"** he or she must Agree to Work for an Average of no less than 4 Hours per Day, or the Equivalent thereof, for 6 Days per Week: beCause we have a LOT of Work that needs doing, just to Build those **"GLORIOUS Swanky Hotels Castles and Fortresses,"** which will Require about 6 Years of Labor, just to Build the Hotels and Fortresses. Therefore all such Working Soldiers will be Keeping their Promises, and Cheerfully so: beCause of Visualizing their New Life within such Beautiful Places. Indeed, there will be a Danger of them Overworking themselves: beCause of being Anxious to get the Work Finished, and therefore perhaps do a Bad Job of it: beCause of being too Tired. Therefore, getting them to Limit themselves to only 4 Hours of Work per Day will no doubt be a Big Problem. Actually, with the Correct Equipment to Work with, most Concrete Projects can be Finished within less than 4 Hours, in which Cases those Working Soldiers could have the Remainder of those Days Off for Playing Games, Reading, Cooking, or doing whatever they Want to: beCause we are NOT going to be Running any Slave Labor Camps. But, we will Try to get the Heavy Work done during the Cool Times of the Day: so that no one must Work during the Heat of the Day, unless the Work is Inside of some House, where it is Cool and Comforting for Working, or Warm and Comfortable, depending on the Weather.

04-07 [_] So, O Elected King, it is Obvious that you Think and Plan such Things as if you Actually were the Elected King with an Unlimited Supply of Money to Work with, which is Unrealistic: beCause none of those Lying Zionist Red Jews, who now Control the Money Supply, will go along with you and **The Worldwide People's Revolution!®** Indeed, they are likely to get some Nation Stirred Up for going to War Against you and your Revolutionaries. ‡

04-08 [_] Well, we have no Plans for Fighting them in any War. Therefore, it would be Cold-blooded MURDER in the First Degree. After all, if any of my Proposals seem to be Unjust to those Red Jews, they are Welcome to Prove it at: **"The Great Worldwide TELEVISED Court HEARING!"** However, I dare say that not one of those Spiritual COWARDS will Show his nor her Face at that Great Meeting of the Most Intelligent Minds: beCause **"The Swanky Sword of Divine Truths"** is on our Side. Therefore, they cannot Win in a Courtroom with Law and Order, with a Righteous Judge in Charge of it, having all of the People in the World for a Jury, who can Vote for whether or not they Want to Establish **"The New RIGHTEOUS One-World Government,"** or go on living in their States of Extreme Poverty! Indeed, they Presently do not have Fresh Clean Air to Breathe, Pure Living Water to Drink, Wholesome Natural Foods to Eat, nor Secure Houses to Live in, much less any **"GLORIOUS Swanky Hotels Castles and Fortresses"** with **"Beautiful Swanky PALACES!" (A New Concept in Living Habits — Palaces for Poor People!)** By The Worldwide People's Revolution!® ‡

04-09 [_] O Elected King, I just cannot Believe that anyone in the World would be Willing to do any Work without being Able to OWN his or her own Private House, Garden, Workshop, Sales Shop, Indoor Swimming Pool, 5,000$ Pool Table in a Game Room, Theater, Gymnasium, Tennis Court, Bowling Alley, Ice-skating Rink, Concert Hall, hundreds of Fruit Trees, Waterfalls, a River of Living Water, Flower Gardens, Vegetable Gardens, Vineyards, Wine Cellar, Root Cellar, Walk-in Cooler, Walk-in Freezer, Canning Kitchen, Juicing Machine, Sewing Machine, Gold-plated Rolls-Royce Car, Helicopter, and Private Jet Airplane. Indeed, most People who have the American Dream would Want a Big Wooden Mansion on the Hilltop with 4 Garages, and a Fleet of Limousines, just in Case they Want to Show Off their Riches to their Frendz and Naaberz. Therefore, once they have Dreams like that in their Heads, it is Unlikely that they are going to be Contented to Own nothing more than Combs, Toothbrushes, Fingernail Trimmers, Telephones, Computers, Books, and some Fine Hand-crafted Furniture, which might Require 40 Years to Obtain it: beCause of having to Wait on some Trees to Grow for making Lumber. †§‡

04-10 [_] Well, do you Believe that the President of the United States would be at all Interested in Moving himself and his Family into some little Shack in Mississippi with Nigger Jim and Huck Finn? Indeed, if you gave to them the Choice between Living in the White House, in Washington, or Moving into that 2-Bedroom Shanty in Mississippi, there is a ZERO Chance that they would Willing Choose to Live in that Shanty, even if they could Afford to Buy it: beCause they are already Spoiled by the Luxuries of the White House, which would be the same Thing for those Voluntary Working Soldiers, who would have no Desire to Leave their **"Beautiful Swanky PALACES,"** nor any Reason to Leave them, if they Built them: beCause, if they are Built Correctly, those Palaces will be in Good Shape 10,000+ Years later: beCause of taking Good Care of them, which will not Require much Care, if they are Constructed According to my Instructions: beCause there will be NO Metal to get Rusted Out, nor any Exposed Stone Domes, whereby the Weather might Damage them. Indeed, even the Half-dome Granite Stone Entrances will be Protected by Overhanging Ceramic-tiled Roofs, just to keep the Acid Rains Off of them. Moreover, some of those Kinds of Roofs have already Endured for thousands of Years, which is Proof that they Work Well. Another Option is to use Sheets of Glass to Cover those Entrances. Therefore, if any Parts do Wear Out — such as the Granite-faced Floors, they will not be Wearing Out during our Lifetimes. ‡

04-11 [_] So, O Elected King, a Person would have to be a PROUD Ignorant FOOL to Reject your Master Plan, and Choose to Live in some Ugly Shanty or Firetrap Mouse-infested Cockroach Den, when they could Choose to Live in **"Beautiful Swanky PALACES,"** which they could Live in for as long as they might Want to, and then Move to other Swanky Palaces, whereby they could get to Tour the World! After all, it would not Require much Effort to Pack up any Personal Belongings, and Move Out, if one did not Own much of anything. Therefore, would that Plan not Destabilize the Masses of People, who would not have Permanent Places to Live: beCause of Moving all about on the whole Earth, just to Smell the Fragrant Flowers, here and there, and Eat the Exotic Fruits, here and there, and Visit the Swanky Castles, here and there? Indeed, it would be like the President Moving into some Castle in England or Ireland, just to Experience the Pleasures of it at Royal Swanky Buffets! ‡

04-12 [_] Well, rather than become Destabilized, I would say that they would at last get Stabilized, and thus Settle Down in their Favorite Places with their Best Frendz and Naaberz, who might even Move Together as a Group of Wise People, or even go to Work and Build New Houses for themselves. After all, the Heavy Equipment would be doing most of the Hard Work. Therefore, Young People might get Inspired to make Better Plans, and thus Build Better Palaces, after Seeing a lot of Swanky Palaces. Yes, they might Study them for any Faults, whereby they could make Improvements, with the Approval of **"The New RIGHTEOUS One-World Government,"** which would naturally have the most Professional Architects, Designers, Engineers, Construction Generals, and so on.

04-13 [_] O Elected King, I am Worried that we might Run Out of Rocks to Work with, if we are not Careful: because not all Rocks are Good for Building Swanky Palaces. ‡

04-14 [_] Well, that is just another Good Reason for Establishing **"The New RIGHTEOUS One-World Government,"** which will have to Inventory all such Mountains of Rocks. I am told that most of the Himalayas are Limestone; but, *Wikipedia* offers no Proof of it. However, it does state that about 16% of the Rocks in the Crust of the Earth is/are Granite. Therefore, we are not

(The Equitable Wage System!)

likely to Run Out of Granites to Work with, which are the Hardest most Enduring Building Stones, even though some of them are Radioactive to some Degree; and therefore, they might not make Good Dome Homes; but, there are many other Uses for them, such as Paved Walkways, Elevators, Stairways, and Places where People do not spend much Time. ‡

04-15 [_] So, O Elected King, it Appears that if the Printing Presses of **"The New RIGHTEOUS One-World Government"** do not break down, we will be Financially Able to do just about anything that we might Imagine, just as long as it is Approved by the Government Architects, Engineers, Geologists, Designers, Environmentalists, and other Professionals.

— Chapter 05 —

No more Debts

05-01 [_] Lying Zionist Red Jews will no doubt Object to my Proposal to Forgive all Debts, Return the Lands to the People, and Celebrate the Great Year of JUBILEE: beCause that would Mean that they would not be Collecting a Trillion Dollars or more per Year for Interest Payments on their Loans, Worldwide, for doing almost nothing. However, there is no Group of People on this Earth who can more Rightly Afford to Forgive all such Debts, than those Lying Zionist Red Jews. Nevertheless, if they Sincerely Believe that they have a Just Cause for Collecting all such Usury, they are Welcome to Present their Arguments at: **"The Great Worldwide TELEVISED Court HEARING,"** where they will be in Danger of being Sentenced to 40 Years of Hard Labor in Rock Quarries, if they are found to be Liars, Deceivers, Greedy Hogs, Selfish Dogs, and General Psychopaths, who have little Empathy for Poor People, who will Divide the Bankers' Spoils among them, Legally: beCause we are going to Do as Moses Taught, and Celebrate the Year of JUBILEE at Bankers' Expense. After all, if Moses had it WRong, how come none of those Jews have written any books that reveal the Evils of the Laws of Moses, beginning with Forgiveness and Restitution. Indeed, if it were Chief Jews who had been so Mistreated, I am Sure that we would have Heard about it by now. Strangely enough, the Laws of the Land seem to be in Favor of those Lying Red Jews, and not in Favor of Poor Honest White Jews, nor of any of the Working Class of People, who are Expected to Pay that Usury and the National Debts: beCause we supposedly Owe it to them, just beCause they got to Manage the Printing Presses that Produced the Money that we, the People, supposedly Borrowed — Thanks to the Military Industrial Congressional Bankers' Complex, which is Neatly and Deliberately Arranged in Favor of Zionist Red Jews, which is easy to Prove in a Courtroom, if anyone Doubts it. ‡

05-02 [_] O Elected King, why not just Hang all of those Lying Red Jews, and be Done with them, without bringing them to Court: beCause it would only be a Waste of Time, since they already Confess, and even Brag about being the Richest People in the World, who most Certainly did not Gain their Wealth by Honest Labor of any Kind; but, they got their Wealthies by Financial Stealthies, by Cunning Financial Devices, by Stock Options, Derivatives, Deceptions, and Lies — even as Donald Trumpeter Gained his Wealth by Bankruptcies, by not

Paying his Workers, by Stiffing them, by Cheating, by Lying, and whatever was Necessary to get more Money: beCause he is the Perfect Example of a Capitalist HOG, who is another Lying Red Jew at Heart, if not by Blood. †§‡

05-03 [_] Well, Donald has been Better at Playing the Capitalist Game, than many Capitalists; but, none of his Property will be Worth anything when all such Cities of Confusion are Abandoned for the most Part, even as it was in Detroit, Michigan. After all, *"there shall be many Great and Fair Cities without an Inhabitant"*: beCause the People will be moving into those **"GLORIOUS Swanky Hotels Castles and Fortresses,"** at least if they are Wise, just to Collect those FAIR Swanky Wages, if nothing else, even if they cannot Tolerate the Beauty that will Surround them. (See *Jeremiah 4:7; 9:11; and 34:22,* and Related Verses.)

05-04 [_] O Elected King, if those Stone Dome Home Complexes are not Built Correctly, they will be Cold Damp Humid Moldy Stinking Places to Live. Indeed, those Stone Domes will be Collecting Moisture, much like Caves, which are Musty and Dangerous Places to Live: beCause they are Unhealthy.

05-05 [_] Well, the Solution to that Problem is found in your own Statement — all such Stone Dome Homes must be Built Correctly, which is to have ICE HOUSES under them, which are used to SUCK UP the Moisture that gets into the Dome Homes, Workshops, and Sales Shops, which the Normal Person could never Afford; but, it is no Problem for **"The New RIGHTEOUS One-World Government,"** which will have an Unlimited Amount of New Money for Hiring it to be Done, Correctly. Indeed, the ICE will Attract the Moisture, just like a Glass of Cold Water with Ice in it, which Sweats. Therefore, during the 3 or 4 Hot Summer Months, those Ice Houses will come in very Handy, which I have already Explained in some other Book, for which I have forgotten the Name. However, if you Search for it, you can Find it.

05-06 [_] O Elected King, the Pantheon in Rome does not have any Ice House under it, and yet it has never Suffered with Moisture, Mold, nor any other Detrimental Thing, in spite of getting about 7 Million Visitors per Year. ‡

05-07 [_] Well, we can Check it out when we Hold **"The Great Worldwide TELEVISED Court HEARING!"** Moreover, we can Check out the History of Saint Peter's Basilica, as well as other Buildings that are Self-air-conditioned, whereby we can Discover just how BAD they are. However, I would be Willing to BET that "Wherever there is a Will, there is a Way," as the Old Saying goes, even if that Way has not yet been Discovered by us. Indeed, someone has no doubt already Discovered it, who can Reveal it at that Great Meeting of the Most Intelligent Minds.

05-08 [_] O Elected King, I must Confess that such a Great Meeting will Prove to be most Interesting, if your Plan is Followed, even if no Swanky Fortresses ever get Built: beCause it could be that everyone will Decide to Build and Live in those **"Beautiful Swanky PALACES!"** Yes, they could even be Built Outside of Present Cities of Confusion, if there is Space for them.

05-09 [_] Well, the Fortress Plan would still have to be Followed, or else certain Advantages would be Lost — such as Keeping Out any Unwanted Varmints, Criminals, Politicians, Wicked Lawyers, Greedy Medical Doctors, Stinking Prostitutes, Drug Pushers, and so on. Moreover, if

(The Equitable Wage System!)

the Palaces were not Built HIGH above the normal Ground Level, on TOP of Swanky Cisterns, there is a Chance that those Palaces could be Flooded with Water; and especially if they are Located in Low Places — such as Houston, Boston, Los Angeles, Miami, London, and so on. Indeed, even the Great Plains are in Danger of being Flooded. ‡

05-10 [_] O Elected King, do you Sincerely Believe that it might be Possible to Keep Out the Drug Pushers, seeing that we are still using that Filthy Money, which we should get RID of, and use RFID Computer Chips, only?

05-11 [_] Well, I have no Interest in any Radio Frequency ID Chips: because I would Choose to Live in a Swanky Fortress where everyone is Familiar, and everyone has Chosen to Willingly Live without any such Drugs, even as I have Lived my entire Life without them. Moreover, I am not at all Tempted to Try them: beCause I have a Natural "High" all of the Time!

05-12 [_] O Elected King, that is very Good of you; but, we cannot Expect Immature Teenagers to be so Self-disciplined. Therefore, it will Require Moats and Tall Stone Walls around those **"GLORIOUS Swanky Hotels Castles and Fortresses!" (Beautiful Planned City States for WISE Intelligent Well-Educated People with Common Sense and Good Understanding!) By The Worldwide People's Revolution!® Book 019.**

05-13 [_] Well, there is still the Possibility that someone will Think of a Better Solution when we hold that Great Meeting of the Most Intelligent Minds; but, I Doubt it: beCause those Swanky Fortresses are God's Way of Solving all such Problems. Indeed, the Drug Pushers are simply Banished. ‡

05-14 [_] What if some Baby Christian is Seduced and Enticed by some "Friend," to Try using Drugs for the Great Thrill of it, and then Invites that Baby Christian to Visit some City of Confusion where the Drug Trafficking is Flowing, even as it is right now in many American Cities — HOW will you Prevent the Addictions of all such Children?

05-15 [_] Well, it will Depend on the Willpower of the Parents, who should Love their Children enough to Protect them from all such "Friends." After all, it will be easy to Protect them, simply by not giving their Children Permission to Leave their Fortresses: beCause there will be no such Drugs within any First Class Swanky Fortresses. In Fact, if someone is Discovered Using such Drugs within those Fortresses, there is a Good Chance that they will be made into SLAVES in Rock Quarries for Punishments: beCause, if they Want to Use Drugs, they only need to Check the Box [_] with an X.

    A-[_] I do NOT Want to Use any Illegal Drugs.

    B-[_] I Promise to NOT Use any Illegal Drugs.

    C-[_] I will not Knowingly Use any Illegal Drugs.

    D-[_] Marijuana will not be Illegal in Seventh Swanky Fortresses. Therefore, if I Want to Use it, I Understand that I will not be Punished for it.

E-[_] I can Live a Healthy Happy Life without the Use of any Drugs, Alcoholic Drinks, nor even Cokes and other so-called "Soft Drinks," which are also Addictive.

F-[_] I Prefer to get "High" on Spiritual "Trips" with God, by Means of Fasting and Praying, which is Harmless, Uplifting, Self-rewarding, Beneficial, and Godly. {See: **"HOW to Become a HOLY Man!" (40 Good Reasons WHY People Should FAST and PRAY!) By The Worldwide People's Revolution!® Book 045.**}

G-[_] I Believe that God Created all Things, including Natural Drugs, for us to Use Wisely for Treating our Ailments.

H-[_] I Honestly have no Idea what is Good for me; but, it is for Sure that I do not have to make myself into a Guinea Pig for Testing Drugs, which have already been Proven to be BAD, which have Caused many Unnecessary Deaths. Therefore, I am not going to make my Body an Experimental Drug Dump, like the Cigarette Addicts have done, who have already Proven how BAD those Stinking Cigarettes are. Nothing was Gained by Using them, except to Teach to us how BAD they are, which is WHY no such Drugs will be Found in the Holy Kingdom of All that is GOOD, which is the Kingdom of God. ‡

— Chapter 06 —

WHY the War on Poverty FAILED

06-01 [_] First of all, those Lying Red Jews did not Want to get Rid of Poverty: beCause they Thrive on it. Indeed, would anyone go to a Friendly Banker to Borrow Money, if they were NOT Poor? Of course not! They go to Bankers to Borrow Money: beCAUSE of Needing more Money for Buying a House, Car, Tools, Furniture, or whatever: beCause that is HOW those Greedy Red Jews have Set it Up. Indeed, they could have Obeyed the Laws of Moses, and not made Usury Slaves, Interest Slaves, Work Slaves, Childcare Slaves, nor Tax Slaves of anyone, even as I have Revealed in Chapter 03-07—12, which any 12-year-old Intelligent Child can easily Understand. Yes, please do yourself a Great Favor, and Discover such a Child, and have him or her Read those Verses, just to Discover the Truth of it. ‡

06-02 [_] O Elected King, with God's Economic Plan, which you have Accepted, there would be no Need for any Bankers, Insurance Slave Masters, Medical Doctors, Pharmacies, Drugs, Reformatories, Prisons, Police DEPARTments, nor Automobiles! Therefore, we would be Bored half to Death without any Rapists, Thieves, Liars, Robbers, Drug Addicts, and other Victims of Capitalism. Yes, I just LOVE those Bloody Gory Car Accidents, Plane Crashes, Train Wrecks, and all such GOOD Things, which are almost as Good as those Gory Wars, whereby the Guts of Healthy Young Men are Spilled on the Ground, which gives to me a Good Appetite to EAT and get DRUNK, and Enjoy the Glories of Capitalism! And I am NOT Crazy! †‡§§

(The Equitable Wage System!)

06-03 [_] I Heard a Report on C-SPAN, which Revealed that American Tax Slaves have now Wasted more than 22 Trillion Dollars on "The War on Poverty," which Poverty is now Worse than ever, whereby there are more Poor People in **"The Divided States of United Lies,"** now, than ever before: beCause the War on Poverty has utterly Failed with a Capital F. However, WHY did it Fail? Obviously it was NOT a War against Poverty, or else the First Attack would have been Against those Lying Red Jews, who are the Chief Proponents of Poverty, who Love it: beCause they Collect no less than a Trillion Dollars per Year for Interest on LOANS to the Governments of the World, beginning with **"The Divided States of United Lies!"** Yes, it is very Profitable for them to Pretend that they are Helping us, by Loaning more and more Money to us Ignorant FOOLS, when no such Loans are Needed, even as was Proven in Chapter 03-07—12.

06-04 [_] O Elected King, I Hear what you are saying; but, at the same Time, I am Greatly Perplexed about it all: beCause I cannot Imagine Living without Bankers, Insurance Agents, Government Welfare Programs, and all of those Wonderful BureauRATS in the District of Criminals, in Washington, who Grease the Wheels of Capitalism, who keep the Money Flowing in Endless Streams of Living Waters, you might say: beCause of Borrowing Money from those Friendly Banksters, who Control the Printing Presses that make the Money, as well as the Computers that keep Track of it. Yes, your Hebrew God has me Bewildered: beCause I cannot Comprehend the SIMPLICITY of a RIGHTEOUS GovernMint, which has an Unlimited Amount of New Money, which must be Earned by Honest Labor, without any Loans, without any Interest, and without any Taxes! Yes, it is Mind-boggling to Think about it: beCause it is Contrary to everything that we have ever been Taught, beginning in **"The Public School of IGNERUNT FQLZ!" (HOW we have been GRAATLEE DISEEVD!) By The Worldwide People's Revolution!®** Book 024. Yes, the Idea of almost everyone Living in their own Manmade Garden of Eden, in **"Beautiful Swanky PALACES,"** is simply Mind-boggling, and Far Beyond my Ability to get my Mind Wrapped Around it. Are you saying that it might be Possible for Lawyers, Judges, Policemen, Firefighters, Medical Doctors, Prison Keepers, Politicians, Preachers, Teachers, and all such People to be Contented to Live in **"The Environmentalists' Paradise"** with Huck Finn and Nigger Jim, who Attend to their Gardens, Vineyards, Orchards, and Home-craft Workshops? Would that not be far too SIMPLE? †§‡

06-05 [_] Well, X-amount of those People would have to Learn HOW to do Construction Work, and Properly so: beCause we have those **"GLORIOUS Swanky Hotels Castles and Fortresses"** to Build. Indeed, those Burly Policemen and Firefighters could become Stone Masons, and thus Retire their Pistols in Swanky Armories and Museums: beCause they will no longer Need any Weapons: because nearly everyone will be Cheerfully going to WORK, Building those Beautiful Planned City States for WISE Intelligent Well-Educated People with Common Sense and Good Understanding! Yes, the Unemployment Rate will be ZERO, and Worldwide!

06-06 [_] O Elected King, I now Understand WHY you are our Elected King — it is beCAUSE you have a Real Workable and Reasonable SOLUTION for Low Wages and Unemployment! However, are you Sure that the World will not be FLOODED with far too much Money, whereby People will be Buying MORE of those Stinking Noisy Polluting Gas-hog CARS? Indeed, they will all be Wanting Stretched Limousines, like Michael Jackson's, as well as all Kinds of other Vain Things — such as Grand Pianos, Pipe Organs, and even their own Private Saturn V Rocket Launchers for Visiting the MOON! †§‡§§

06-07 [_] Well, they will be Encouraged to Buy their own Stone Dome Home Complexes with their Extra Money, or else Save their Money for the Time when they Retire at 36 Years of Age, when they can Tour the World, and Discover Beautiful Things to Buy, and take those Things back Home with them, in order to Enhance their Swanky Palaces, which will Increase with more and more Wealth and Beauty, until at last they will all become Richer than normal Kings and Queens! After all, none of them will have to Buy their own Stone Dome Home Complexes, if they do not Want them: beCause those **"GLORIOUS Swanky Hotels Castles and Fortresses"** can and should Belong to **"The New RIGHTEOUS One-World Government,"** which will make it Possible for everyone to Prosper in a RIIT WAA, at Home, without Running Around and Around like Chickens with their Heads Cut Off. Indeed, many of those Wise People will then come to Understand the Inspired Words of Jesus Christ, who said: *"Do not Think that a Man's Life Consists in the Abundance of his Possessions: because there is much more to Life than Collecting all Kinds of Vain Things, which the Wild Animals Live Happily without, and are Contented with all such Good Things, who get to Enjoy the Beautiful Things in Nature, even the Sunrises, Sunsets, Rainbows, Awesome Clouds, Fragrant Flowers, Majestic Trees, and other Wild Animals — none of whom have made themselves into Tax Slaves, Usury Slaves, Debt Slaves, Insurance Slaves, Drug Slaves, Childcare Slaves, nor Work Slaves: beCause they are Free with a Capital F, and Enjoying every Minute of it. Yes, they often Quote a Good Poem, called: 'HOW Could We Afford It?'*

> A-[_] Suppose that our Great Creator God Charged us for the Rain, or put a Price on the Songbird's Strain — on his Cheerful Music, at the Dawn of Day, or on the Mist on the Great Plains — how much would Autumn Landscapes Cost, or a Window that is Etched with Winter's Curious Frost, or the Glory of the Rainbow that is so Quickly Lost?
>
> B-[_] Suppose that People had to Pay, in Order to Watch the Deers and Antelopes Play?
>
> C-[_] Or, just to See a Crimson Sunset while Listening to the Master Farmer say: *"Yes, suppose that People had to Pay for a Sky that is Full of the Majestic Stars of the Milky Way, or for the Waving Flags of the Colorful Northern Lights, whose Glory should make you Humble during those Special Nights? Suppose it were 500$ per Night, just to Watch the Pale Moon's Silvery Light, Dancing behind Fluffy Clouds, which seldom if ever Draw any Crowds? What would it be Worth to Watch a Sea Gull in Graceful Flight, who Navigates about without any Fright? And what about the Artic Crane, who Flies from Pole to Pole without any Great Strain, who Bypasses Hurricanes and Storms on the Great Sea: because of having Marvelous Brains?"*
>
> D-[_] How much, I wonder, would it be Worth for Prisoners of so-called Civilized Societies to Smell of the Good, Brown, Fragrant Earth — during Springtime — the Miracle of Births?
>
> E-[_] How much do you Think that People would Pay for a Baby's Laugh at the Close of Day, after they have Slaved Away all Day for their Taxes to Pay?
>
> F-[_] How much could the Great Creator God Charge us for the Multitudes of Flavors of Foods and Drinks, which no one has ever Numbered for their Endless Varieties, when

(The Equitable Wage System!)

Combined with Spices for Ungrateful and Unthankful Fools, who just Assume that all such Things Created themselves — by Chance, Luck, and Circumstance?

G-[_] Yes, suppose that the Master Farmer Charged us for them, I say — what would be the High Cost of Living, during these Days, and Especially if nothing were Giving, and all were Getting — like those Lying Selfish and Greedy Red Jews of the Synagogue of Satan, who will Falsely be Accusing the Colorful Peacock from Angel Ridge of Satanic Slander?

H-[_] Suppose that we Paid to Look at the Rolling Green Hills, for the Rippling Mountain Rills, or for the Mating Song of the Western Meadowlark, whose Voice no Man can Speak of with a Bad Remark; or, suppose we had to Pay for Sweeping Breakers of the Sea, for their Grace, Awesome Power, and Majesty?

I-[_] And yet, all of those Good Things the Generous Creator and Marvelous Inventor GIVES TO US, for FREE — for Beauty to Behold, for Love, Respect, and Glory to Impose, even from the most Colorful and Fragrant Rose!

J-[_] Now, therefore, Count the Cost, O Humble Children of the Great King, and do not say that you are Poor, and cannot Sing: because you have much more than any of those Herds and Birds, and you could all be Spiritually Rich with these Inspired Words from the Master Farmer and Chief Judge!

K-[_] How much would we Pay for Healthy Working Muscles, for a Brain that does not Forget, and for a Heart that seems to never Quit, in spite of Working both Day and Night without any Pay, you might Say! Yes, Thank God that our Feet are Willing to Walk, and our Backs are Willing to Bend, and both of our Hands are Willing to Understand HOW to Work, and do not Complain with a little Dirt, nor even with a little Hurt!

L-[_] Yes, the Train of Thoughts is running along the same Track, which could possibly go on and on, even Across the Great Plains that Stretch Out across the Imaginative Mind, which Visualizes Palaces of Peace in the Blest Land of Perfect Oneness, where the Little Birds of Cheerfulness are Singing, and the Fragrant Flowers are Blooming all about the Lovable Courts of King Solomon, you might say; but, as Jesus Christ said: *"You shall Learn the Great Truths that I Teach, and those Truths will Set you Free when you Practice them. Therefore, if you are Free, you must be Free in Deed with a Capital F, even as I am Free and Ready to Fly Away to Mount Zion."* — The NMV

M-[_] Money is the Principle Tool of a Righteous GovernMint. Therefore, it must not be put into the Evil Hands of Greedy Selfish People; but, it must be Used Wisely for making all Honest Hardworking People Moderately Rich, without any Loans, without any Interest, and without any Taxes, which is not very Poetic; but it Rhymes with all other Truths in the Good Books, which can easily be Proven in a Courtroom with Law and Order, with a Righteous Judge in Charge of it. Therefore, how much is such a Judge Worth to the Children of Poverty and Shame, who could be Living in **"Beautiful Swanky PALACES,"** just by Exercising their DUMBmocracy — by Speaking Up for the Great Truths that he Teaches, whereby they might Elect him to be their Righteous

King, by putting his Name on the Election Ballot. However, why have any such Election, at all, if no one Opposes him: beCause of not being Able to Fight Against **"The Swanky Sword of Divine Truths!"**? Indeed, would that not also be another Waste of Money, Time, Materials, and Energy?

06-08 [_] O Elected King, suppose God Charged us for Oxygen, at the same Rate that Hospitals Charge — HOW could we Afford to Buy anything else? Thank the Great Creator God that everything in the Natural World is in Perfect Harmony, whereby the Earth is Designed Perfectly for the Establishment of **"The New RIGHTEOUS One-World Government!"** Yes, the Natural Resources are Distributed in such a Way around the World, whereby True Justice cannot be Served without such a Good Government. For Example, Saudi Arabia might have lots of Crude Oil; but, it Sorely Lacks Mountains of Good Building Rocks. However, with some Cooperation, they could Exchange their Oil for some Rocks, which they should do right away, before the Oil Industry is Retired to the Trash Dump with Capitalism, Communism, Socialism, Fascism, and any other False Economic Systems, which Ignore the Fact that this World was Designed for a Righteous One-World Government, only. †‡

06-09 [_] Well, many Nations, including Saudi Arabia, will just Naturally Object to the Establishment of any such One-World Government, on Account of their Religious and Political Beliefs, which they are Unwilling to Defend at: **"The Great Worldwide TELEVISED Court HEARING!"** Indeed, Saudi Arabia would be one of the First to Object: beCause Visitors, for Example, are not even Welcome in Mecca, unless they are Muslims! Imagine how they would Feel, if the Israelis said, "Only Jews are Welcome in the Land of Israel. No Muslims, Hindus, Buddhists, nor Christians are Allowed." HOW would that Closed-mindedness Bridge the Gap between them and other Religious People, whose Beliefs might be just as Good as their own? You can Bet that their Money would be just as Good in any Country, including Saudi Arabia, who would likely Sell their Oil to whomever might Pay for it, at their Price, which should be FREE, just like the Rocks in the Rocky Mountains of **"The Divided States of United Lies,"** which would also not Want to Join **"The New RIGHTEOUS One-World Government,"** under the Great Pretense that Americans are Better than other Peoples, just beCause they were Born HERE, instead of over THERE, which somehow Glorified Americans, who still Vainly Imagine that they are Living in "the greatest nation on the earth," they say. However, after the Atomic and Hydrogen Bombs fall on them, and Wipe them Off of the Earth for their WICKEDNESS, they might have to Adopt a New Song, and Confess that it is ONLY by the Grace of God that anyone is even one Degree Better than anyone else in any Way; and that same God Wants all of us to Love our Naaberz as much as we Love ourselves, which would Begin with a Confession that our Naaberz are Equally as Worthy of Fresh Clean Air, Pure Living Water, Wholesome Natural Foods, and **"Beautiful Swanky PALACES,"** as we are, and Especially if they are as Innocent as those little Brown Baby Jesuses, who only Want an Opportunity to Earn an Honest Living, without making themselves into Future Tax Slaves nor Interest Slaves of some EVIL Empire, which takes Advantage of them, just beCAUSE they Happen to be Born into a Family of Lying Zionist Red JEWS, who most Certainly have a Shameful Superiority Complex — Thanks to the Inspired Words of an Unholy Mutilated BIBLE, which Deliberately Sets them Up Above all other Nations, in Order to TEST their Spirits, in Order for God to Discover whether or not they are Humble and Honest, or Proud Liars. Indeed, if they were Humble Honest Servants of God, they would be the First to DEMAND **"The Great Worldwide TELEVISED Court HEARING,"** whereby it might be Discovered WHO the True Servants of God ARE — and they

(The Equitable Wage System!)

are NOT Lying Greedy Selfish Red Jews, who have the Capacity to FORGIVE all Debts, and thus Celebrate the Great Year of JUBILEE! Yes, Moses and Elijah will Set the House in Order!

06-10 [_] O Elected King, when you Consider the FACT that all of those Lying Red Jews can REPENT, and thus become Honest White Jews, who can go to Work and Build their own **"Beautiful Swanky PALACES,"** it does not make any Sense that any of them would Object to the Establishment of **"The New RIGHTEOUS One-World Government!" (HOW to Establish a Righteous One-World Government without Going to WAR!) By The Worldwide People's Revolution!®** Book 056. Indeed, they have nothing to Lose, except their Pride and Vanity; while they have all to Gain by Cooperating with you and **The Worldwide People's Revolution!®**

06-11 [_] Well, those are my Exact same Sentiments — they have all to Gain in the Way of Righteousness, and nothing to Lose by Cooperating, and Cheerfully so: beCause New Yuck City is the Primary Target of their Enemies, who have every Justifiable Cause on their Side for such an Attack. In Fact, all of the Nations will Gang Up Against them, if they are not Wise: beCause of taking Advantage of them for so many Years, and in all Ways, while making Drug Addicts of them for more Unholy Gain: beCause almost everything that they Say and Do is for Financial and Material Gain. Therefore, it is now Time for them to come Clean, and make Full Confessions of all of their Sins, and Do what is RIIT for all of the Peoples, including those Poor Palestinians, American Indians, Africans, Asians, Europeans, Indigenous Peoples, and whomever they have Mistreated and taken Advantage of. Indeed, Normal Americans are their Chief Victims, and do not even Know it: beCause of having their Minds Blinded by such Songs as, *"God Bless the USA,"* which has a Line of Lies, like this: *"I'm Proud to be an American, in the Land of the Free!"* Yes, they Vainly Imagine that they are Free with a Capital F, when they are nothing more than Tax Slaves, Interest Slaves, Insurance Slaves, Drug Slaves, Childcare Slaves, Sex Slaves, and Work Slaves, who are now more than 20 Trillion Dollars in Debt to those Lying Zionist Red Jew Sons of Satan!

06-12 [_] O Elected King, if I were you, I would round up all of those Lying Red Jews, bring them Trials, and Crucify everyone last one of them, or else Stuff them into those Nazi Crematory Ovens, if they did not make their Confessions and Restitutions. Moreover, I would not Permit them to Build any Swanky Palaces for themselves: because they are Unworthy of them. †§‡

06-13 [_] Well, those Zionist Jews can be very Thankful to God that I am not you. Moreover, I Seriously Doubt that there are enough of them to Fill even one Swanky Palace, even though there are Red Jew Sympathizers by the Millions, who should also be brought to Court and put to Open Shame, just for Seeking to Justify their Evil Ways. After all, there would not have been any Second World War, nor even a First World War, if it had not been for those Lying Red Jews and their Zionist Friends and Sympathizers, who also Seek to Justify the EVILS of Capitalism, without even Counting how many Evils there are! Yes, those Stinking Noisy Polluting Automobiles would be a Good Example for them to Study, while Tides of the Oceans are Rising at their Heels, which could Drown the District of Criminals, and New Yuck City, Lungdung, Honk Konk, Moscow, and other Red Jew Centers of Corruption. {See www.Amazon.com for: **"The Nature of CAPITALISM!" (A List of the EVILS of CAPITALISM!) By The Worldwide People's Revolution!®** Book 038.}

06-14 [_] O Elected King, I Drive a nice Quiet Cadillac, which does not Pollute the Earth in any Way: beCause it gets 20 Miles per Gallon of Gas, even with the Air-conditioner running. Indeed, I get to sit for at least 2 Hours in very slow-moving Traffic, while I work my way to Work each Morning, and then repeat that same Process during the Evening Rush Hour, which gives to me Time to Think. Yes, I am an Upper Class American, who can Afford such a New Car; but, I have Noticed that most of the Cars are not Quiet, and most of them are Spewing Out their STINK, as you say, which is especially True in Poor Countries, where 99% of the Cars are Old and Un-tuned and True Abominations in the Nostrils of your Hebrew God, which is especially True of their Pickups, Buses, Trucks, Tractors, Trains, and Airplanes, which would not even be Legal in **"The Divided States of United Lies!"** Moreover, guess WHO is the Least Capable of Paying a Fine for having such a Bad Vehicle, in America? — the Poor Person who Owns such a Vehicle, who cannot Afford a Tune-up, Repair Bill, Insurance, nor anything: beCause he is POOR, and Working for almost Minimum Wages at 2 Jobs, just to Feed and Clothe his 6 Children, who have no Garden to Work in, who are Addicted to Eating Expensive Chips and Dips, whose Mother weighs no less than 350 Pounds (158.75 kg), and has a 20-pound Tumor inside of her, which Begs for Expensive Drugs, just to keep her Alive, after Eating no less than a whole Chicken each Day, or 2 Pizzas, some Iced-cream, Cookies, and a dozen Cokes: beCause she is also Addicted, and has no Idea what to Do about it. Nevertheless, she does manage to Clean the House, Wash the Clothes, Manage the 2 Babies, and Watch TV. Indeed, she Hates to read books, and Loves the Comedies, whereby she might Distract her Mind from the Realities of Living. Meanwhile, her Husband is making as many Sacrifices as he can, and does his Best to Obey the Civil Laws, and keep his Bills Paid; but, behold, if he gets an extra Dollar, it must be Spent on Capitalist Shoes, New Tires, Medicines, or something: beCause he has Fallen Headlong into the Bottomless Pit of Capitalism, which is Full of Poisonous Lying Snakes, you might say, who have no Empathy. Yes, even the Church has taken up Donations for him and his Family, and the Food Bank has Helped them out; but, no matter what, there is no Way that he will ever be Able to Afford to Buy one of those Electric Hybrid Cars, whereby he might Stop Polluting the Earth so much. Nevertheless, having a Living Conscience, it does Bother him that he is Contributing to the Destruction of the Earth — that is, to the Destruction of the Air, Rainwater, Rivers, Lakes, Oceans, and Lands around the World, all of the way to Alaska and Patagonia: beCause that is **"The Nature of CAPITALISM!"** †§‡

06-15 [_] Well, my Friend, all such Poor People should Especially be Interested in Living in those **"Beautiful Swanky PALACES,"** except that they Lack any Faith in it, who must be Encouraged by all Means available to have Faith: beCause they are most Desperate, and also most likely the most Honest and Hardworking People, who have simply been the most Deceived. ‡

(The Equitable Wage System!)

— Chapter 07 —

Flushing Money Down the Drains

07-01 [_] Now, just Try to Imagine how many of those **"GLORIOUS Swanky Hotels Castles and Fortresses"** could have been Built by Wisely Using that 22 Trillion Dollars that was Wasted on the "war on poverty" Nonsense. First of all, we, the People, could Claim our own Mountains of Rocks, Sand, Gravel, Water, and other Building Materials: so that we would not have to BUY our own Air and Water, etc., and then we could have Used that Money Wisely for HIRING **"Seven Great Armies of Working Soldiers"** to Build their OWN **"Beautiful Swanky PALACES!" (A New Concept in Living Habits — Palaces for Poor People!) By The Worldwide People's Revolution!®** That Way, at least 100,000,000 Americans would have been "Fixed for Life," with an Average of 220,000$ per Person! ‡

07-02 [_] O Elected King, I will be Happy to Work for only 10$ per Hour, if I can get to move into one of those **"Beautiful Swanky PALACES,"** just as soon as we can get it Finished. Moreover, I would say that 22 Trillion Dollars would Buy all of the Necessary Tools for putting every Young Person in the whole World to Work for 10$ per Hour, who would also be Happy to move into their own Swanky Palaces.

07-03 [_] Well, I would say that you are Correct. After all, that is a HUGE Amount of Money; and those Ignorant Politicians have Plans for Wasting more Money than that during the next 20 Years, and will still not have any Good Things to Show for it! ‡

07-04 [_] O Elected King, I would say that if a Family were Set Up as you Propose, having a one-acre Organic Garden, Walk-in Cooler / Freezer / Root Cellar / Storage Domes, 4 one-million-gallon Cisterns for Water Storage, a Spacious Kitchen, and all of the Well-made Tools to Work with, they would be Moderately Rich, and even Richer than Bill Computer Software Gates, who does not have such a SECURE Stone Dome Home Complex to Live in, who would be Judged to be an Extremely Poor Person, when Compared with those **"Seven Great Armies of Working Soldiers,"** who would have the Best Foods and Drinks in the World, which Bill has most likely never Tasted: beCause of knowing nothing about **"The LUSCIOUS All-Mineral Organic Method of Gardening!" (HOW to Grow DELICIOUS Satisfying Foods for Potential Kingz and Kweenz in Swanky PALACES!) By The Worldwide People's Revolution!®** Book 021. Indeed, not even the Queen of England has had it so GOOD! †‡

07-05 [_] Well, you have likely been Privileged to Taste of some Good Fruits and Vegetables; but, most Americans have not, and especially if they are Young: beCause one cannot Discover any such Foods in the Gross Grocery Stores. Therefore, what seems to be Good to you, is not necessarily Good to them: beCause they have been Greatly Deprived of the Better Things in Life. However, almost everyone can Remember having Tasted of *something* that was Exceptionally Good to them, which will be more and more the Case as we get those Beautiful Planned City States Built, and the Gardens Growing.

07-06 [_] O Elected King, talk about Flushing Money Down the Drain, just Think of all of the Trillions of Dollars that have been Wasted on Medical Care, Wars, Drugs, Insipid Foods, Poisonous Drinks, Cosmetics, Perfumes, Household Cleansers, Paints, Solvents, Gasoline for Automobiles, Diesel for Trucks, and Jet Fuel for Airplanes, which were never Needed for True Prosperity: beCause those **"GLORIOUS Swanky Hotels Castles and Fortresses"** can Function Perfectly Well without any of those Things, and every Family could have their own Grand Electric Piano / Organ / and 100+ Instrument Keyboard, like you have probably seen for Sale for 10,000$ in some Shopping Maul in **"The Divided States of United Lies!"** Yes, the Children could all be Healthy and Happy without any of those Motorcycles, Motor Scooters, Snowmobiles, Cars, Vans, Busses, Pickups, Trucks, Tractors, Lawnmowers, Weed-eaters, Chainsaws, Hedge Trimmers, Leaf Blowers, Garden Tillers, Shredding Machines, Dangerous Chemicals, Deadly Sprays, nor any Trash that is Produced by the Capitalist Hogs, which has Filled Up Trash Dumps all around the World, as well as Contaminated the Oceans from Coast to Coast, all around the World — Thanks to the Great False Economy. {See: **"The Great False Economy is now DEBUNKED!" (Adolf Hitler had a much Better Economic System!) By The Worldwide People's Revolution!® Book 053.**}

07-07 [_] Well, I Prefer **"Are Americans the Most STUPID People who ever Lived?" (HOW Working People can PROSPER and Live in PEACE Under the Rulership of a RIGHTEOUS KING!)**, Book 047, plus: **"The UGLY Scarred Dishonest Face of Poor Old Miserable UNCLE SAM!" (A Memorial Day Legacy!)**, Book 054, plus: **"The Loathsome Burdens of the Independent Jackasses!" (A New Approach for Solving our Massive Problems!) By The Worldwide People's Revolution!® Book 051.**

07-08 [_] O Elected King, I have been Thinking about the Trillions of Dollars that have already been Wasted on Disaster Reliefs — such as Hurricanes, Tornadoes, Floods, Fires, Mudslides, and Earthquakes — not to Mention the Unnatural Disasters, such as the Nuclear Power Plant Disasters in Russia, Japan, and wherever. Why is it that People cannot Understand that they are Setting themselves Up for all such Disasters by NOT Building those **"GLORIOUS Swanky Hotels Castles and Fortresses!"**?

07-09 [_] Well, no matter how many Bad Things Happen to them, very few of them come to any Rational Conclusions: beCause of Lacking VISION, which is the Ability to Foresee what is Coming, or what might Come. For Example, if you Lived in a very Windy Place, WHY would you Think of Building a Paper House, like the Japanese might do? Likewise, if you Lived in a Low Swampy Place, like Louisiana, why would you Assume that you could not or would not get Flooded Out? Indeed, anywhere along a River has the Potential of Flooding, even if your House is 100 Above the River: beCause you never know what might Happen Upstream, and even hundreds of Miles Away. Likewise, if you Built a House below a Big Barren Hill, or along some Cliff, you could Expect a Mudslide and the Loss of your Home. Therefore, why be a Fool? Why not Study: **"The Right Design for Living!" (A List of Great Advantages for Building Beautiful Planned City States!) By The Worldwide People's Revolution!®, Book 012?**

07-10 [_] O Elected King, not everyone has Wisdom. Not everyone is Qualified to be an Elected King. Not everyone is Born with a Sense of Riit and wRong. Not everyone has a Good Education, like you have. However, many of them have Graduated from Universities, and still Lack Common Sense, being Thoughtless Creatures, you might say. Therefore, what is to be

Done for them? *"O the Ignorance, the Stupidity, the Unbelief, and the Great Pride of Fools, who Vainly Imagine that they are Wise, just beCause of Learning something, which Puffs Up their Minds."* Yes, it is much Better to be Humble and Perfectly Honest about all Things, including the Living Conditions of other People, most of whom are very Miserable, who Suffer with Bleeding Hemorrhoids, Indigestion, Aches, Pains, Sores, Itches, Fevers, Sicknesses, Diseases, Divorces, Heartaches, Poverty, and you Name it — all of whom could be much Healthier and Happier, if they would only Discipline themselves, and Deny themselves of Vain Pleasures, and take up their Crosses for Following Jesus Christ, who Suffered the Cruelties of Lying Red Jews; but, behold, he Arose from the Dead, and is Alive Forevermore! ‡

07-11 [_] Well, those are Beliefs of tens of millions of People, even if they are among those who are presently Suffering, who often Sincerely Believe that they are like Jobe, who Suffered the Persecutions of Satan, the Devil, which could be True in some Cases: beCause, no matter what they Say nor Do, it all seems to turn out WRong. Indeed, some People call it "Fate," or "Providence." Therefore, if they perceive that they have been Especially Blest, they Credit "Providence" with it; but, if they perceive that they have been Especially Cursed, they Credit it to "Fate," which is Controlled by the Devil. However, there is no Proof of either one being the Actual Case: beCause of a Thing called "Chance," which King Solomon said Happens to all People. (See *Ecclesiastes 9:11*.)

07-12 [_] So, O Elected King, if you become the Elected King of **"The New RIGHTEOUS One-World Government,"** will it be the Work of God, or Satan?

07-13 [_] Well, I would say that it would be the Work of both God and Satan, beginning a very Long Time Ago, whereby everything is now Set Up most Appropriate for the Establishment of **"The New RIGHTEOUS One-World Government!"**

07-14 [_] So, O Elected King, do you Feel as if God were Inspiring every Word that you Write?

07-15 [_] Well, I just Write whatever Words come into my Mind, which seem to be Good to me.

— Chapter 08 —

A List of Swanky Wages for certain Kinds of Work

08-01 [_] To be Perfectly FAIR, Wages must be Paid According to the Amount of Work and the Quality of the Work that gets Done. For Example, it is not Fair to Pay someone the same Wages for Washing Dishes in a Cool Comfortable Air-conditioned Restaurant, as someone who is Setting Heavy Rocks on a Stone Wall during the Heat of the Day, in the Bright Sunlight, who is Sweating Profusely, and is about to Die in the HEAT. Please Check the Following Boxes with Statements that you Agree with, which have your Honest Opinions.

A List of FAIR Swanky Wages!

A-[_] I Agree, it would not be Fair to Pay those Workers Equal Wages: beCause the Stonework is far more Difficult, which anyone would Know for a Fact, if they Tried to do it with a Bad Back. But, even without a Bad Back, it is still Difficult Labor, when Compared with Washing Dishes. Even Heavy Pots and Pans would be more Difficult to Wash, than Plates and Cups, and should therefore Earn Higher Wages.

B-[_] I Believe that the Restaurant might more easily be able to Afford to Pay more Wages than the Stonemason's Boss: beCause of having many more Customers, who often give generous Tips to the Waiters and Waitresses, which should be Shared with the Dishwashers and Cooks, just to be Fair about it.

C-[_] I Confess that the Stonemason would be doing much Harder Work than the Dishwasher. However, he may Prefer to do that Difficult Work: beCause of having the Freedom to do it as he Pleases. After all, there are generally several Bidders on such Jobs; and they can all Agree to Charge more Money for the Work, if they are not Happy with whatever is Offered to them. Moreover, if a Stonemason is Professional, and does Exceptionally Good Work, he can get a Good Reputation, and even become Famous for his Stonework, whereby he can Charge however much Money that he Wants to for his Services, and probably get it, whereas the Dishwasher has no such Reputation, and must make herself into a little Capitalist Slave, just to have a Job.

D-[_] Democracy Demands that they should be Paid according to whatever the Masses of People Vote for: because, by Means of the Internet, we can all now VOTE for Fair Wages, whereby Medical Doctors, Politicians, Lawyers, Professors, and other Professionals can be put into their Appropriate Wage Categories. Therefore, if the Masses of People Vote for Paying a Professor in some College 40$ per Hour for his Services as a Teacher, while Voting to Pay a Stonemason only 20$ per Hour for his Services, then everyone should be Happy with those Wages. After all, the Professor has had to spend much more Time in School than the Stonemason. However, to be Perfectly Honest, I Confess that the Stonemason should be getting 40$ per Hour, and the Professor 20$. †§‡

E-[_] Educated People should receive less Pay for their Services, than Hardworking People: because, without that Hard Work, we would all Starve to Death. For Example, a Poor Ignorant Hardworking Mexican might Receive 2 Cents per Pound for Picking Tomatoes in the Hot Burning Sunlight of Florida, while just Miles away, some Professor might Receive 160,000$ per Year for one-hundredth as much Labor. Therefore, to be Perfectly Fair about it, the Mexican should be Receiving no less than 60,000$ per Year for his Services, while the Professor should Receive no more than 20,000$ per Year: because he does not have to Sweat to Perform his Services. Moreover, the Consumers would only have to Pay 4 Cents per Pound more for their Tomatoes, in order to make it possible for those Mexicans to Receive Good Wages for their Services. Otherwise, those Consumers could Grow and Harvest their own Tomatoes, whereby they might have more Respect for those Hardworking Mexicans, even though no Private Gardener on the Earth, in all of History, has ever spent all Day in the Garden, bending over, picking Tomatoes. Indeed, only Commercial Growers would do that: because no Family would ever Need nor Want a hundred Bushels of Tomatoes to take Care of during just one Day! ‡

(The Equitable Wage System!)

F-[_] I Fail to Understand WHY both Workers are not Paid EQUAL Wages, if they put in Equal Time in the Field or in the Restaurant: beCause it is Possible for the Stonemason to set up a Tent over his Stone Wall, and Work in the Shade with a Fan Blowing on him, which should be the Responsibility of his Employer, if he is Working for some Slave Master. Otherwise, he could Hire someone to Help him to Set Up the Tent, which might Require 40 Strong Men, if the Wind is Blowing. After all, if the Stonework is being done on a Wall that is 210 feet long, it would Require a very large Tent, or Shed Roof, just to keep the Workers Shaded, which could be done with ease if there were **"Seven Great Armies of Working Soldiers"** to Help do the Work, even as it would be, if we were Building those **"GLORIOUS Swanky Hotels Castles and Fortresses!"** In Fact, all of the Work would be done under Shelters, if I had *my* Way; and the Working Soldiers could take Breaks whenever they got Tired: beCause of having FREEDOM. ‡

G-[_] God Knows that it is not Fair to Pay Men Higher Wages than Women for the same Work.

H-[_] HUMBUG! A Big Strong Man can do 10 Times as much Work as a Weak Woman.

I-[_] It seem to me that you Misunderstood the above Statement in Verse G. It does say "SAME WORK." In other Words, if a Woman can Shovel 10 Tons of Dirt into a Wheelbarrow, and Roll that Wheelbarrow up a 100-feet-long Ramp, and Dump it out, every Hour, all Day long, she is Worthy of the same Pay as the Man who can Move 10 Tons of Dirt on the same Ramp, every Hour.

J-[_] Justice Demands that a Pregnant Woman should not be Doing any such Hard Work, lest she should Abort her Baby. Therefore, no Sane Mother would be Doing such Hard Work, no matter what the Pay might be.

K-[_] King Jesus would tell that Woman to Stay at Home, and Attend to her Knitting: beCause she is not Designed to Do such Hard Work, whereby she might Move 80 Tons of Dirt during just one 8-Hour Day.

L-[_] Lots of Laughs! No Man nor Wombman has ever done that much Hard Work during just one Day! †‡

M-[_] How much Money would you like to BET on it? My Brother Vern and I Shoveled and Wheeled no less than 40 Dump Truckloads of Dirt up a 100-feet-long Ramp during just one Week, Working 8 Hours per Day for 5 Days, and never got Paid a Dime for doing it: beCause we got Robbed in a roundabout Way by those Lying Red Jews. ‡

N-[_] Not everyone is so Foolish as you and your Brother, who should have Received no less than 100$ for each Truckload of Dirt that you Moved onto that Roof: beCause of the Steepness of the Ramp, and the Effort that was Required for Moving the Dirt; or, a Total of 800$ per Day, just to be Fair. Moreover, I have never known any Woman who could have Done that much Hard Work, and not have Died from it. ‡

53

O-[_] Are there no OPTIONS? Why not Use a Crane or a Bulldozer for Moving so much Dirt? For Example, a Good Crane could Lift Up the entire Dump Truckload of Dirt, and Dump it Out on Top of the Roof, and one such Truck every 15 Minutes or less! †§‡

P-[_] Many People have tried to Cheat by Using Machines, and have thus Paid a High Price for it. Remember the Crane that Fell Over on a Street in New York City. The Dirt had to be Moved onto the Roof of our Apartment Houses, which were not Designed to be Treaded on by Bulldozers; and a Crane would have Cost no less than 1,000$, just to Move it to the Building Site, plus no less than 300$ per Day for its Services, which would have likely taken 3 Days to get it done. Therefore, we Saved no less than 2,000$ by doing the Work ourselves, by Hand with 2 Wheelbarrows and 2 Shovels and one Long Ramp, which was actually a lot of Fun: beCause of Seeing the Looks on the Face of the Truck Driver, each Time that he Arrived with another Truckload of Dirt, and Caught us in Action, and could not Believe his own Eyeballs! In Fact, he could not Resist the Great Temptation to tell his Boss about it, who also could not Believe it: beCause, HOW could just 2 Men Move a large Truckload of Dirt every Hour, and for 8 Hours per Day, for 5 Days? Nevertheless, it was a True Story, which he Finally had to Accept. †

Q-[_] The Great Question is this: **"Was there no one in the whole County, who was neither Able nor Willing to Help you 2 to get it Done?"** † (It is Bad English.)

R-[_] Well, there was a Republican who Sympathized with us, and a Dimwitcrat who Offered his Bad Advice; but, nobody was Interested in doing it, nor Helping us to do it. Indeed, 2 Big Black Men in their 20's said that they would do it for 1,600$. We said that the entire 2,000-square-feet Rock and Concrete Roof only Costed us 2,000$; and therefore, it would be a little Crazy to Spend 1,600$ just to Move a little Dirt around during one Week. After all, the Roof had no less than 2,000 Wheelbarrows of Concrete and Rocks in it, which had Required 45 Days of Hard Work to Build it, using that same Wooden Ramp. ‡

S-[_] Satan must have been Laughing his Head Off at you 2 Fools! Why in the World would you Seduce yourselves with so much Hard Work, when you could have done much less Work by Inviting a Bulldozer to Mound up some Dirt at the Top of a Hill, Pack it Down in the Shape of a Dome or Igloo, Spread some Black Plastic Sheeting over the Mound, after Shaping it as best you could with some Clay, and then get a Concrete Pump Truck to Cover it with Concrete during just ONE Day, after Pouring a Foundation around the Bottom of the Mound, making it like an Igloo, or Stone Dome Home, and only for about 5,000$: beCause of taking Advantage of Large FREE Rough Rocks at the Rock Quarry? {NOTE: One of my Books gives the complete Details for just HOW to make such a Stone Dome Home for next to nothing, when Compared with a Normal American Wooden / Plastic Firetrap Mouse-infested Cockroach Den, except a LOT of Hard Work during just one Month, in the Springtime, when the Weather is Cooperative. I have Forgotten just which Book it is in; but, I Guarantee it to be there. You can Check Out that Book, or any others that I have written, from your Public LIE-brary, or even from your Church Truth-brary, if they are Wise People in your Community. A Farmer could Trade a Cow or a hundred Chickens for the entire Collection, which would be well Worth it.}

(The Equitable Wage System!)

T-[_] Well, the Total Cost of the Apartments was less than 70,000$, including 2 large Onyx Floors, 9 Agate Windows, and 16 Polished Marble Walls, which Side Walls are 17-feet-thick at their Bases, which makes them somewhat Tornado-proof, you might say, while that 4- to 6-feet-thick Solid Roof with 400 Tons of Rocks is somewhat Hail-proof, you might say. Indeed, just the Fact that the Marble-faced Walls do not have to be Painted, has already Paid for the Houses by the Money that was Saved on Paint and Labor. However, the entire Apartment Houses, the 100,000-gallon 200,000$ Cistern, the 3,000-gallon 5,000$ Cistern, the 10,000$ Bunker / Wash House, the 30,000$ Developed Spring Water House, the 20,000$ Tool House, the 10,000$ Goat House, the 6,000$ Fasting Sanitarium, the 20,000$ Woodshed / Carport, the Special 20,000$ Walled-in Garden, and all of the 40-acre Property was Stolen from us — Thanks to those Lying Red Jew Bankers and their Bursting Housing Bubble Scam. Yes, 30 Years of Hard Work was simply TRASHED!

U-[_] I Understand that you Intend to get Revenge on those Lying Red Jews for their Bursting Housing Bubble Scam; but, there is some Verse about Vengeance belonging to GOD, if I Remember Correctly. So, what about that?

V-[_] Vengeance does belong to God, and God is Bound to Assist me to get it: beCause he Adopted me into his Holy Family, you might say. Therefore, when those Lying Red Jews Crossed me, they Crossed God, which is WHY that they are in BIG Trouble, who will be Vexed unto Death by it.

W-[_] I would say that they will Stir Up another World War, before they will Submit to **"The Swanky Sword of Divine Truths!"**

X-[_] Well, X-amount of People will no doubt Agree with you; but, if War is Required for Correcting them, may the Hydrogen Bombs Soothe their Nerves, and the Alligators Feast on their Rotting Flesh when they Flee to the Swamps of Florida. †§‡

Y-[_] I Believe that I will Yield to the Temptation to Depart from New Yuck City, before those Bombs Drop on them. After all, if any People Deserve to be Cremated Alive, it would be those Lying Red Jews and their Lovers, or whomever Seeks to Justify their EVILS by any Means, including the Making of any Interest Slaves in America. †§‡ {See Chapter 03-07—12.}

Z-[_] The Zeal of **The Worldwide People's Revolution!**® will make it Possible for you to Flee into those **"Beautiful Swanky PALACES!"** ‡

08-02 [_] Super Easy Labor — such as Playing Guard Duty at a Swanky Fortress, while sitting in a Swanky Easy Chair — is worth only 10$ per Hour, which is also a Living Wage for anyone who is Living in a Beautiful Swanky Palace, in Exchange for 4 Hours of Common Unskilled Labor per Day: beCause all of your Expenses are Paid.

08-03 [_] So, O Elected King, would such a Person have to put in 4 Hours of Guard Duty, without any Pay, in Exchange for Living in the Swanky Palace; and then "Work" for 100$ per Hour for Extremely Difficult Skilled Labor for any more Pay?

08-04 [_] No, all Voluntary Working Soldiers, who Join **"The Swanky Associations of Working Soldiers!" (A Fascinating Collection of Various Kinds of Voluntary Working Soldiers!) By The Worldwide People's Revolution!®**, Book 018, would have to put in 4 Hours of Common Unskilled Labor, or the Equivalent thereof, for the Privilege of Living in their Palaces, which seems to be Perfectly Fair to me. However, if you Disagree, please Check one or more of the following Boxes with Statements that you Agree with.

A-[_] I Agree that it is Perfectly Fair, and even Generous on the Part of our Elected King, to Exchange 4 Hours of Guard Duty for the Privilege of Living within **"Beautiful Swanky PALACES!" (A New Concept in Living Habits — Palaces for Poor People!) By The Worldwide People's Revolution!®** Book 066. †§‡

B-[_] I Believe that all of those Working Soldiers should be Charged RENT — such as 15,000$ per Month, just to Help Cover the Costs of those Swanky Palaces, which will Cost no less than a Trillion Dollars for just ONE of those Palaces! †§‡

C-[_] I Confess that all of those Swanky Palaces and Swanky Fortresses could and should Belong to **"The New RIGHTEOUS One-World Government,"** whereby no one would have to Pay any Rent, Property Taxes, Mortgages, Interest on Loans, nor any other Red Jew Scammer's Claptrap Nonsense. After all, if some very PROUD Person Wants to OWN his or her own Multi-million-dollar Swanky Stone Dome Home Complex, including the one-acre Organic Garden, he or she is Welcome to BUY all of it, and thus Slave Away his or her Life just to Obtain it! However, when such a Person Dies, WHO would be Able to Buy it, so as to be Able to Divide the Money among his or her Adopted Children? †§‡

D-[_] When a Person Dies, he or she is Unable to take any Property with him or her; and therefore, Ownership becomes an Obsolete Joke. Actually, Ownership is a Deception of the Devil, which he uses to PUFF UP the Minds of Proud Fools, who Forget that they are about to DIE, even if they Live for 100 Years, which will Fly by more Quickly than most People might Imagine: beCause Life is very Short. Therefore, it is Important that we Learn WHY we were Born into this World, whereby we can make the Best of it.

E-[_] Educated People will not be Playing Guard Duty at any Swanky Fortresses; and therefore, it does not Concern them, whatever such People are Paid for Guard Duty. Therefore, let us get Off of this Subject, and talk about Easy Labor Pay.

F-[_] I Fail to Understand HOW Guard Duty could be Worth any Pay at a Swanky Fortress, since it would be Impossible for 99.999,999,999% of the People in this World of Wonders to Figure Out HOW to Enter such a Strong Fortress, except to go through the Entrance Gates, in Underground Tunnels, which lead to the Swanky Hotels, which might be Miles away from the Entrances, whereby any Potential Criminals could be Trapped. ‡

G-[_] God Knows that such Guard Duty would be Necessary to Watch for ISIS (Israeli Secret Instigation Services), just in case they should Decide to Attack such a Fortress with Stone Walls 200 feet High! Indeed, they would first of all have to Climb over the Outermost Stone Wall, which would be a Minimum of 50 feet Tall, and then let

(The Equitable Wage System!)

themselves down into the Outer Moat, which might be full of Poisonous Snakes and Alligators, and then Swim through that Moat for at least 200 feet, and then Climb Up the Retainer Wall on the inside of the Moat, and then Walk through an Open Field, which might be 1 to 100 Miles in Width, and then Swim through the Inner Moat, which might be a thousand feet Wide, and then Climb Up the Slick Polished Granite Wall, which might be as much as 400 feet Tall at a 33° Angle, and then Climb Up a Steep Polished Stone Wall for another 100 feet or more, and then go around an Overhanging "Cap" on the Top of that Wall, which might Hang Out by 10 to 20 feet, and then go around and over that Cap, just to be Greeted by some very Mean DOGS on the other Side of an Electrified Fence, which has Flares all along it, and Tripwires for setting them Off, along with some Machineguns, which are Designed to Cover all Areas of the Cap with Crossfire: so that only a Rat could pass by without getting SHOT! †§‡

H-[_] HUMBUG! Nobody would go to so much Trouble to KEEP OUT the Israeli Secret Instigation Services (ISIS). After all, they are mostly Unemployed Young Men, who would be Happy to Build their own **"Beautiful Swanky PALACES!" (A New Concept in Living Habits — Palaces for Poor People!) By The Worldwide People's Revolution!®** Book 066.

I-[_] Only Ignorant People would make any Attempt to Enter into a Swanky Fortress Illegally, when almost all of them will have Open Doors within 20 Years, after the Criminals have been Eliminated by Inoculations of Truths in their Ears. ‡

J-[_] Jesus is the Answer. We only have to Believe in Jesus Christ to be Saved from all of our Troubles. For Example, my Aunt Alice is one of those Firm Believers, who was Blown Away in a Tornado, just last Week, and no one has Discovered her Body; but, it was Assumed that the Tornado Deposited her Carcass in the Woods, where she was Eaten by Wild Animals, whereby she was Saved from all of her Aches and Pains by the Grace of God. Yes, she no doubt went to Heaven in a Flying Saucer, which is a Common Thing for True Believers in Jesus Christ. Therefore, just Repent, and you too will be Saved. †§‡

K-[_] King Jesus must not have anything Better to do, than go about Scooping Up his Followers in Flying Saucers. †§‡

L-[_] Lots of Laughs! It is all Religious Superstitious Nonsense! †§‡

M-[_] God have Mercy on you Silly People. Flying Saucers are for REAL. Moreover, if I had enough Money, I would Prove it to you: because tens of thousands of People have Seen them, who could Present their Evidences at: **"The Great Worldwide TELEVISED Court HEARING!"** ‡

N-[_] Not everyone is Interested in any such Nonsense. Indeed, they would rather Learn about Unskilled Easy Labor Wages, which are 20 Dollars per Hour for any Work that can be done while Sitting Down in an Air-conditioned Room — such as Peeling Carrots, Coring Apples, Peeling Potatoes, Trimming Toenails, and so on.

O-[_] I Oppose all such High Wages for such Low Class Workers. Indeed, 15$ per Hour is Plenty of Money for Peeling Potatoes and Carrots, even if it is Boring Work. †§‡

P-[_] Most People would be Contented to Earn 10$ per Hour for Peeling Carrots; but, I would say that 20$ per Hour is Fair: beCause a Lawyer would only get 40$ per Hour for his Skilled Easy Labor in some Air-conditioned Office. Likewise, the Chief Executive Officer (CEO) of any Company would also Receive a Maximum of 40$ per Hour, plus 10$ for the Stress and Responsibility of his Job. ‡

Q-[_] The Great Question is this: **"Is it FAIR to Pay People any Wages, when they are already being Provided with 'Beautiful Swanky PALACES!' (A New Concept in Living Habits — Palaces for Poor People!) By The Worldwide People's Revolution!®?"**

R-[_] Riitlee or Ronglee, I will not Object to any Wages that our Elected King wants to Reward us with: beCause, if I get to Live in a Beautiful Swanky Palace, with Royal Swanky Buffets, in Exchange for only an Average of 4 Hours of Common Unskilled Labor per Day, I will have nothing to Complain about, and will even take up a Study of Religious Subjects — such as, **"In thu Beeginingz uv Thingz!" (Thu Kreeaashun Stooree frum thu Beegining!) By The Worldwide People's Revolution!®**

S-[_] I Prefer the Skilled Difficult Labor Wages — such as 80$ per Hour for Laying Heavy Granite Stones, which Weigh no less than 70 Pounds, each, which Require 2 Strong Men just to Lay them on a Stone Wall, whereby I can Build Up my Beautiful Muscles, whereby I can have Better SEX, which Means more to me than all of the Money in the World! †§‡

T-[_] The Size of my Tally Whacker means more to me, and all of that Hard Labor will make it Shrink Up, like those of Weight Lifters, who have a Difficult Time Discovering it in their Underwear, as was the Case with Arnold S. and Donald T., who could not Satisfy their Women. †§‡

U-[_] I Understand that it is Possible to Live and Work at Home, once we get those Swanky Fortresses Finished. For Example, we only need to do 4 Hours of Common Unskilled Labor, making Carrot Juice, Apple Juice, 100% Mango "Iced-cream," or whatever is Needed by **"The Swanky Associations of Working Soldiers,"** and then we can have the Remainder of the Day for ourselves, to do whatever we Want to do, including Earning Swanky Wages — such as Helping to Build a Swanky Cathedral at the Swanky Castle, whereby we might Earn 50 to 120 dollars per Hour, depending on the Skill and Labor involved. †§‡

V-[_] You are a Victim of Religious Deceptions: beCause there is no one on the Earth who could Afford to Pay 50 to 120$ per Hour for any such Work. †§‡

W-[_] Well, you Suffer with Welfare Disease, whereby you Vainly Imagine that Governments cannot Create Jobs, in spite of the Fact that **"The New RIGHTEOUS**

(The Equitable Wage System!)

One-World Government" will be the Chief Employer in the World, if I have MY Way, and I am the Elected King of **The Worldwide People's Revolution!®**

X-[_] X-amount of People will likely Learn what you are Proposing, and Brand you as a Neo-Nazi, Communist, Socialist, or a New Kind of Capitalist with a Tale of Lies a Mile Long. Yes, they will be saying that you are Anti-Semitic, a Racist, and a DICTATOR, even though I cannot Recall any Dictations to Obey. After all, everyone is Free to Choose to Live in **"Beautiful Swanky PALACES,"** or in their Wooden / Plastic Firetrap Mouse-infested Cockroach Dens, which are not Fit to Live in, which are nothing but Eternal Expenses, while those Swanky Palaces have ZERO Expenses: beCause they are Designed for LIVING! Yes, it is the *"Back to Eden" Plan.* Therefore, it is now Time to get to Work at it. †§‡

Y-[_] I am Severely Tempted to Yield to the Great Temptation to BURN my Wooden / Plastic Firetrap House, if the Leaders of the World do not Agree to Attend **"The Great Worldwide TELEVISED Court HEARING!"** Indeed, it will be my Way of Saying that I have had all of the BILLS that I Want, which the Federal Government will Eventually have to Agree with, and Especially if my Burning House just Happens to Catch some others on Fire, whereby the entire City of Confusion is TRASHED, come next April 19th. After all, the Burning of the Branch Davidians, in Waco, Texas, was a Good Example to Imitate, even if a few People Die from it; and I am not Insane. †§‡§§

Z-[_] It does seem like your Zeal could Drive you Insane. This must be a Peaceful and Non-destructive Revolution, in order to be Successful. Therefore, come next April 21st, the Members of **The Worldwide People's Revolution!®** can simply go to BED, and Stay in Bed, until the Leaders of all Nations Agree to DEMAND **"The Great Worldwide TELEVISED Court HEARING,"** whereby we can Treat this Subject in a Civilized Manner, with Law and Order, with a Righteous Judge in Charge of the Court, whomever that Judge might be — it matters not to me: beCause all that I am Concerned with is Learning the WHOLE TRUTH about all Important Subjects, beginning with the Evil Events of September 11th, 2001, the HoloHOAX, the MoonHOAX, the Kennedy Assassination Cover-up, and the Secret Workings of the Military Industrial Congressional Bankers' Complex Economic System, whereby we Tax Slaves and Interest Slaves are now 150 Trillion Dollars in DEBT to Lying Red Jew Banksters! Otherwise, if they are Innocent, let them Prove it. Yes, let them Prove that World Trade Center Tower 7 IMPLODED ITSELF without the Use of any Controlled Demolitions. {See the Internet for: www.AE911TRUTH.org for the Proof that it was a False Flag Government Operation. Search for *Experts Speak Out,* and *Dr. Judy Wood* on YouTube Videos.}

08-05 [_] Unskilled Common Labor Wages for Picking Fruits, Hoeing Weeds in a Garden, Washing Dishes, Cleaning Houses, and Herding Goats is worth no less than 50$ per Hour, plus 10$ per Hour for Incentive Pay for Working in the Heat or Cold. However, if you Disagree, please Check the Appropriate Boxes below, which have Statements that you Agree with.

A-[_] I Agree that if anyone is Willing to do any of those Jobs, or any Jobs like them, they should be Paid no less than 50$ per Hour, if they do Good Works, and do not Hoe

Off the little Plants, for Example, which is easy to do, if one is Careless, or loses Concentration on his Work.

B-[_] I Believe that those Wages are FAIR, just as long as everyone in the World is Receiving the same Wages for the same Work.

C-[_] Contrary to Popular Beliefs, it is Possible and most Practical if there are NO Wages Paid for any Services: beCause it is far more Efficient to use **"Seven Great Armies of Working Soldiers,"** whereby each Army has its Responsibilities. For Example, one of those Armies can be Responsible for Growing the Foods and making the Drinks, while another Army can be Responsible for making the Tools to Work with, while another Army can Build the Railways and Tunnels and Pipelines for Transporting the Mountains of Rocks, Sand, Gravel, Water, and whatever is Needed; while another Army can Build those **"GLORIOUS Swanky Hotels Castles and Fortresses!" (Beautiful Planned City States for WISE Intelligent Well-Educated People with Common Sense and Good Understanding!) By The Worldwide People's Revolution!®** Book 019. Yes, another Army can make all of the Clothing and Uniforms for all of those Swanky Armies, one of which will Specialize in Producing Beautiful Ceramic Tiles: beCause each of the one-million-gallon Cisterns for Water Storage must be Lined with Ceramic Tiles, just to make it Possible to Clean them: beCause CLEANING is a Major Occupation, which will always be Needed. Therefore, we must Learn HOW to make that Cleaning EASY. †§‡

D-[_] What about DEMON-ocracy? Will we not be Free to CHOOSE whether or not to Live in Clean Houses or Dirty Houses? Will some Swanky Association of House Cleaners be coming around once per Week to Mop and Sweep the Ceramic Floors throughout all Swanky Fortresses: beCause that is their SERVICE, in Exchange for Living within Beautiful Swanky PALACES! (A NEW Concept in Living Habits — Palaces for Poor Ignorant People, who are too Stupid to make Capitalist Toys to SELL!) By **The Worldwide People's Delusion!®**? †§‡§§

E-[_] Educated People will not Object to Contributing only 4 Hours of Unskilled Common Labor, or the Equivalent thereof, per Day, 6 Days per Week, in Exchange for getting to Live in those **"Beautiful Swanky PALACES!" (A New Concept in Living Habits — Palaces for Poor People!) By The Worldwide People's Revolution!®**

F-[_] I Failed to get through High School, and did not even Want to go to High School to begin with: beCause I was Able and Willing to go to Work when I was only 12 Years Old. Therefore, if I could have Lived in a Swanky Palace in Exchange for only 4 Hours of House Cleaning, per Day, I would have Gladly done such Work, and spent the Remainder of the Day Reading the Bible, or some other Good Book — such as: **"The New MAGNIFIED Version of The Book of MOORMUN!" (The Story of the White and Dark Indians in the Americas!) By The Worldwide People's Revolution!®** ‡

G-[_] God Knows that you were a Good Boy, and would have done Well in Life, no matter what Kind of Work that you might have Chosen to do in your Home-craft Workshop: beCause you were Blest with Special Gifts; but, not everyone is so Blest. ‡

(The Equitable Wage System!)

H-[_] HUMBUG! Anyone can set his or her Mind on a Special Skill, or even Invent a New Skill, and Earn a Fine Living in Life, if they are Set Up with the Basic Necessities of Life, which Begin with those Swanky Stone Dome Home Complexes, all of which must have Gardens, Vineyards, Orchards, and Home-craft Workshops with Well-made Tools.

I-[_] Innocent Children will be Able to Maintain their Innocence with our Elected King's Master Plan: beCause they will not be put Under the PRESSURE of having to Figure Out what they are going to Do when they Grow Up: beCause they will be Raised in their Gardens and Home-craft Workshops, which will also be near to other Gardens and Home-craft Workshops, where they will no doubt Discover what Kinds of Work that they Like Best. Yes, their Naaberz and Frendz will be Inviting them to Visit their Houses, where they will just Naturally Discover Beautiful Things, which will Inspire them to make Similar Things, or even Simple Things like Brooms, Bushes, Mops, and Robes.

J-[_] Justice Demands that all of the School Children are taken on Tours of other Swanky Fortresses, where they might Discover Potential Friends and Soul Mates, and even Live with them, if they Love them, whereby they can Learn New Skills. After all, that is what Freedom is all about. †‡

K-[_] King Jesus would go down to Egypt, and spend 12 Years there, waiting for that Wicked King Herod to DIE, before coming back Home to Nazareth; and then he would never Mention the Great Pyramids, Treasure Cities, nor anything that was Found in Egypt; but, if it had been me doing those Things, I would have had much to Say about Egypt. Therefore, that Part of the Biblical Story is Obviously just another Red Jew LIE! ‡

L-[_] Lots of Laughs! King Jesus never got anywhere near Egypt, and was so Ignorant that he did not even know when Figs should Bear Fruits; and therefore, he Cursed a Poor Fig Tree, which would have been Happy to have been Blest with Ever-bearing Figs, if he had only Blest that Tree, instead of Cursing it, which could still be Bearing Sweet Figs, the Year Around, which would have been Proof that Jesus Christ Actually LIVED! †§‡§§

M-[_] MONEY was the Motive. Indeed, Jesus did everything that he did for the Sake of Gaining MONEY: beCause he was a Distant Relative of Donald Trumpeter and Hilarious Clinton; but, not Burn Me Sanders, who should have been Wise, and taken up **"The Swanky Sword of Divine Truths!" (The Most Powerful Weapon in the Whole Universe!) By The Worldwide People's Revolution!® Book 065.** †§‡

N-[_] Donald Trumpeter is a near Relative of Rudely JEWleeonee, the X-mayor of New Yuck City, who was in Charge of Things during September 11th, 2001, whose Office was Located in World Trade Center (WTC) Tower 7, who was a Good Friend of Lying Larry Silversteen, who should be Prosecuted for their Criminal Acts, and for the Murders of whomever Died by and for those Evil Events. Trust me, "Like Father, Like Son," is the Old Motto for Rudely Jqleeonee. †§‡

O-[_] I am Opposed to calling People Dirty Names, even if they are Dirty People without Consciences, who Profess to be "Christians," and use such Catch Phrases as, "God Bless America."

61

P-[_] Politicians will say and do almost anything to get Elected, if they Believe that it will Gain them some Votes. However, Peacocks are NOT Politicians, nor Preachers; but, they are Inspired Authors of Good Books, which have a Positive Side and a Negative Side. Therefore, we just have to Learn to Keep our Eyes on the Positive Side, and not be Distracted by any "Name Calling" that other People do.

Q-[_] The Great Question is this: **"Could any Person in his or her Riit Miind Object to Earning 50 Dollars per Hour for Unskilled Common Labor?"** If so, he or she should be Horsewhipped! After all, that is no less than 200$ for only 4 Hours of Labor, which will easily Buy 4 Roasted Chickens and a Bag of Potatoes. †§‡

R-[_] I have no Idea HOW anyone could Rightly Complain about such Good Wages. After all, if a Person Wanted to, he or she could easily Earn 400 per Day, or 2,000$ per Week at that Rate, and soon Buy one of those 10,000$ Grand Pianos!

S-[_] SILENCE is much Better than NOISE. Indeed, the Heart is made Better by Silence. Therefore, let the whole Earth keep Silent: so that God might Speak. {See www.Amazon.com for: **"God Speaks and the Whole World Listens!" (Fire on the Mountain from the Burning Bush by the Spirit of Truth!) By The Worldwide People's Revolution!® Book 026.**}

T-[_] Time will Prove that those Swanky Wages are not even Needed, if we Build those **"GLORIOUS Swanky Hotels Castles and Fortresses!" (Beautiful Planned City States for WISE Intelligent Well-Educated People with Common Sense and Good Understanding!) By The Worldwide People's Revolution!®** Book 019. Indeed, most People will say, "To Hell with Money — what do I Need with MONEY?" After all, if they Want something to Eat, they will only have to move their FAT Overstuffed Bodies to a Royal Swanky Buffet, where they can Eat all of the Foods and Drinks that they might Want, for FREE, just as long as they have done their 4 Hours of Common Labor per Day — such as Picking Fruits from Trees, and Berries from Bushes: beCause **"The Swanky Association of Wheat Farmers,"** for Example, will be Harvesting 20 Million Bushels of Wheat per Hour from their Wheat Fields, with Normal Combines, in spite of any Pollution that they might put out: because that is what Gasoline is Good for; but, NOT for Running 2 Billion Cars around on Endless Highways: beCause that is a Waste of Gasoline. Therefore, that must STOP. ‡

U-[_] You must Understand that a Machine can do the Work of 10,000 Strong Young Men. Therefore, those Combines and Bulldozers will come in Handy for Building Swanky Fortresses, and Harvesting Foods, which will be FREE for **"The Swanky Associations of Working Soldiers!" (A Fascinating Collection of Various Kinds of Voluntary Working Soldiers!) By The Worldwide People's Revolution!®** Book 018. Therefore, when there is an Abundance of Good Foods to Eat, People Eat much less of it; and therefore, they are less Fat, and more Healthy and Happy. But, when People are Deprived of Good Foods, they are Hungry all of the Time, and can never be Satisfied. {See: **"DIETS!" (A Reasonable Solution for the "Eternal Controversy"!) By The Worldwide People's Revolution!®** Book 037.}

(The Equitable Wage System!)

V-[_] Queen Victoria would have Loved it!

W-[_] Warmongers and Moneymongers will not Love it; but, they can go Straight to Hell with Satan, the Devil.

X-[_] X-amount of People will not Like it at first; but, after Discovering all of the Good Things that will be Produced by **"The Swanky Associations of All-Mineral Organic Gardeners,"** they will Learn to Love it.

Y-[_] I am Inclined to Agree with you: because I have Yielded to the Temptation to Buy some of those Wholesome Natural Foods, whereby I have Learned that they are more Satisfying than Chemicals and Water.

Z-[_] The Zeal of **The Worldwide People's Revolution!**® will make it all Possible.

08-06 [_] Skilled Common Labor — such as Setting Tiles on a Wall, Laying Bricks, and Cooking — is worth at least 60$ per Hour, if it is done Correctly and Professionally. For Example, a Professional Tile Setter can Set 10 Tiles or more per Hour, depending on the Circumstances. The most that I have Set is 144 one-foot-square Marble Tiles during one Day. However, it was only a Fair Job, and not a Good Job, much less an Extremely Good Job: beCause it was a New Occupation for me. Nevertheless, most People would not Notice the Faults in my Work, unless they were Pointed Out. Getting all such Tiles Set Perfectly is almost an Impossibility: beCause the Tiles are not always Cut Perfectly the same. Ceramic Tiles are often more Accurate; but, not always Trustworthy.

A-[_] I Agree that it is Difficult to make anything Perfect, even if you are Professional. Some more-professional Person can likely find Faults with it. For Example, this Book could be more Professional; but, it would Require much more Time to get it that Way, and nothing much would be Gained by it.

B-[_] I Believe that this Book is Good enough for the Purpose that it Serves, which is about FAIR Swanky Wages, which would be NO Wages at all, if God had his Way: beCause everyone in the World would be Living in those **"Beautiful Swanky PALACES,"** which would be their Fair Wages for the Work, even though the next Generation of People who Inherited all such Palaces would not have to do any Work to Build them; but, only to Maintain them, who should still be Happy to do 3 or 4 Hours of Work per Day, just to keep everything Working Well, as a United Family. Indeed, there would be Houses to Clean, and Windows to Wash without any Stinking Windex; but, possibly with a little Vinegar in the Wash Water. Moreover, there would still be Gardening to do, Canning Foods, Freezing Foods, Drying Fruits, Gathering Nuts, Making Up Beds, Washing Clothes, Cooking, and Washing Dishes — that is, IF the People did not go for Eating only RAW FOODS, as all Animals do, which would Save a lot of Time and Effort; but, it would not be as Pleasurable, unless those Raw Sweet Juicy Fruits were really GOOD, which they can be and should be.

C-[_] I Confess that I am not very Good with Skilled Labor — such as Setting those Marble Tiles on the Walls; but, I am still Able and Willing to Work HARD at whatever

Needs Doing. Therefore, I would Volunteer to do Difficult Unskilled Labor — such as Shoveling Sand or Gravel all Day long, which is Worth at least 70$ per Hour, plus Incentive Pay for Working during the Heat of the Day, or during very Cold Weather, even though Cold Weather is normally no Problem: beCause of Working so Hard. However, if I did not Collect any Incentive Pay for Working in Cold Weather, it would be Fair for me to Collect TWICE as much Incentive Pay for Working in very HOT Weather. In other Words, I could Earn 80$ per Hour for Working during the Heat of Summer, as soon as the Temperature rises over 90 °F (32 °C); and 90$ per Hour when it rises over 100 °F (37.7 °C), no matter what the Humidity might be: beCause that is the Reason for getting 70$ per Hour, with the Assumption that the Weather is Humid. However, if someone does not Believe that such Pay is Fair, they should Volunteer to do Common Unskilled Labor, or Common Skilled Labor, or some Indoors Work of some other Kind. However, most Outdoors Work can be done during the Cool Time of the Mornings, and then everyone can Rest for the Remainder of the Day, unless they have Sheds to Work Under in the Shade, and perhaps Fans Blowing on them. Whatever the Case, everyone should be Happy with whatever Work that they are doing, or else find Different Work to do, which **"The New RIGHTEOUS One-World Government"** will Help them to Discover: beCause, after going through "Basic Training," most of the Work will seem to be Easy: beCause of those Working Soldiers Building Up their Beautiful Muscles. ‡

D-[_] Can we not Exercise our Democracy, and VOTE for our Wages?

E-[_] Educated People might Want to do that, with the Assumption that there might be something Gained by it; but, the Bottom Line in this Case is NOT Money: beCause the Money is actually the Least of our Concerns: beCause, once almost everyone is Living in Swanky Palaces, of what Interest will Money be, seeing that Communications and Transportations are also FREE, being Provided by **"The Swanky Association of Communications and Transportations!"**? Indeed, you will not have to Rent a Room at any Swanky Hotel, if you Belong to **"The Swanky Associations of Working Soldiers!"** Therefore, being a Member of those Associations, you will also be Able to Eat all that you might Want at Royal Swanky Buffets, and get any Clothes or Uniforms that you might Want at Clothing Stores. Otherwise, you could make your own Clothing, if you Wanted to. I have done it for more than 40 Years. However, each Swanky Army will have its own Special Uniforms for Parades, Church Services, Schools, and whatever. Therefore, if you made some Non-uniform Clothing, it would only be for Wearing at Home, or whenever you Leave your Fortress for Visiting the "Outside World," or New York City, for Example, whereby you would not be Identified as a Working Soldier; but, just as another Civilian Idiot, who has not Discovered the Blessings of Uniformity and Conformity to Unity, which calls for a Humble Attitude toward Clothing, which is often the Reason for someone's Destruction: beCause "Civilian Clothing" has a tendency to Build Up PRIDE, which comes before Destruction. Indeed, an Innocent Child, who is Dressed in Expensive Clothing, which is Noticeably Better than the Clothing of the other Students in School, may begin to Vainly Imagine that he or she is Better than the other Students, whereby he or she may Despise or Look Down on them as being Inferior, which is not Good: beCause the Clothing of a Peacock does not make him one Degree Better than any Ordinary White Chicken, Black Chicken, Brown Speckled Chicken, nor any other Chicken: beCause it was only by the Grace of God that such a Peacock was

(The Equitable Wage System!)

Blest with such a Colorful Tail, for which he should be most Thankful; but, NOT Proud of it: beCause that could get him Killed. However, if all of the Children are Dressed like Colorful Peacocks, none of them will Feel Superior among themselves, alone; but, if they go Visiting other Schools, where the Children are not so Colorful, they might Vainly Imagine that they are Better: beCause of their Clothing. Therefore, it is my Honest Opinion that all Clothing should consist of ROBES of Plain Colors with Trimmings of Darker Colors. For Example, Light Green Robes should have Dark Green Trimmings. First Graders could Wear Light Brown Robes with Dark Brown Trimmings, while Second Graders could Wear Orange Robes with Dark Brown Trimmings, while Third Graders could Wear White Robes with Dark Brown Trimmings, while Fourth Graders could Wear Light Green Robes with Dark Green Trimmings, while Fifth Graders could Wear Yellow Robes with Bright Green Trimmings, while Sixth Graders could Wear White Robes with Dark Green Trimmings, and so on. There are perhaps a thousand or more Combinations of Colors to Choose from. ‡

F-[_] I Fail to Understand what is WRong with everyone Wearing whatever Clothing that their Parents Want them to Wear, until their Parents Die; and then they can Choose whatever they Want to Wear. †§‡

G-[_] God Knows that such Parents would be making their Children very Unhappy by Denying them of the God-given Right to Wear whatever Colors and Kinds of Clothing that they Want to.

H-[_] HUMBUG! Those Children would never know the Difference, if no one Mocked them for whatever Kinds and Colors of Clothing that their Parents Dressed them with, or even Failed to Dress them with, as they might do in Africa, in the Jungle, where almost everyone goes Naked. Why not just have ALL of the Children Dressed in White Robes with Blue Trimmings from Grade One to Grade 12, and then let *them* Choose whatever Colors and Kinds of Clothing that *they* might Want to Wear? †§‡

I-[_] Innocent Children might not Object to that Plan; but, Teenagers are likely to Discover Different Clothing on the Internet, and thus Lust after it, as if they could Improve on the Clothing that was Worn by Jesus Christ, who Wears ROBES. (See *The Book of Revelation* for the Proof.)

J-[_] Justice Demands that all Working Soldiers should be Dressed in UNIFORMS, whatever they might be: beCause it is Important to be Able to Recognize WHO Belongs to **"The Swanky Association of Architects and Engineers,"** for Example, who should have Special Uniforms: beCause they are Special People with Special Professions. Likewise, Medical Doctors and Nurses should have Special Uniforms: so as to make it easy for People to Recognize them, which is WHY Policemen Wear Special Uniforms. Therefore, there is nothing Wrong or Evil about that — except that it DIVIDES People into CLASSES, whereby certain Uniformed People will just Naturally Assume that they Belong to the UPPER Class, which will just Naturally PUFF UP their Pride, and make them Vainly Imagine that they are Better than the Lower Classes of Gardeners, Cooks, and Clothes Makers. †§‡

K-[_] King Jesus would Dress everyone in the SAME Uniform, which is WHY John wrote that he saw a Great Multitude, who were Dressed in White Robes. (See *Revelation 7:9* in several Versions.)

L-[_] Lots of Laughs! King Jesus had a Golden Girdle about his Loins, which Identified him as the KING of Kings: beCause he Believes in RANKS, Kings, Priests, Prophets, Pastors, Preachers, and Professors, who are like Different Parts of a Body. Therefore, each Part must be Dressed Differently: beCause there is a lot of Difference between the Functions of the Liver and Lungs, not to Mention the Brains and the Heart. Therefore, all of that Great Multitude, who were Dressed in White Robes were only the SKIN of the Body of Christ, which is the Largest Organ of any Body, if you Study it. †§‡

M-[_] People with Money should be Able to Wear whatever Kinds and Colors of Clothing that they Like. However, if you are Attempting to Form some Religious CULT, you will Naturally Need Uniforms: so as to SEPARATE the People into CLASSES, whereby one Class can Rightfully HATE the other Class, just like most Americans HATE those Greedy Selfish Bankers, who should have to Wear Black Robes with wide Yellow Stripes down their Backs, and Bright Red Crosses on their Chests, just to Warn People of their GREED! †§‡

N-[_] Not everyone Wants to Wear any Clothing at all; but, most People do: beCause they are Ashamed of their Nakedness, even as they should be. However, I would like to Live in a Nudist Colony.

O-[_] Are there no other OPTIONS to Choose from?

P-[_] Most People will Cheerfully Submit to **"The Swanky Sword of Divine Truths!"** Therefore, if our Elected King says that we should Wear Robes of Various Colors and Kinds: beCause of the 77+ Good Reasons and Great Advantages for Making them and Wearing them, then it is Best to SUBMIT: beCause it is Good to be Modestly Dressed.

Q-[_] The Great Question is this: **"What does our Clothing have to do with FAIR Swanky WAGES?"**

R-[_] Well, it Actually has much to do with it, if we are Identified by our Clothing — that is, if our Occupations are Identified by our Clothing, whereby a Republican can be Identified from a Democrat, and a Rat from a Cat, if you know what I Mean. However, in this Case, with Swanky Fortresses, it is most Important to be Able to Identify which KIND of a Swanky Fortress that a Person is Associated with: beCause they come in Degrees of Righteousness, whereby the First Kind is the Most Righteous of the Seven Kinds. Therefore, they should Wear nothing but White Robes, even if they have Blue Trimmings: beCause they are supposed to be HOLY People. {See www.Amazon.com for: **"HOW to Become a HOLY Man!" (40 Good Reasons WHY People Should FAST and PRAY!) By The Worldwide People's Revolution!® Book 045.**}

S-[_] Saints should Wear White Clothing to Identify them from Sinners, who should Wear Darker Clothing, according to the Degree of their Sins. Therefore, all Members of

(The Equitable Wage System!)

the SEVENTH Swanky Fortresses should Wear BLACK Clothing, or at least Black Robes, even if they Wear White Underwear. Therefore, a SIXTH Swanky Fortress should be Dressed in BROWN Clothing; and a FIFTH Swanky Fortress in GRAY Clothing; and a FOURTH Swanky Fortress in GREEN Clothing; and a THIRD Swanky Fortress in YELLOW Clothing; and a SECOND Swanky Fortress in BLUE Clothing; and a FIRST Swanky Fortress in WHITE Clothing, no matter what Colors their Trimmings are. Indeed, the Teachers could Wear White Robes with Red Trimmings, or Yellow Robes with Red Trimmings, if they are Spiritual Cowards to some Degree. Indeed, someone needs to make up a Book concerning this Subject. ‡

T-[_] Time will Prove that most People will be Unhappy with Government Dress Codes, unless they get to Choose their own Kinds and Colors of Clothing. However, I say that everyone should have Different Kinds of Clothing for Different Occasions. For Example, when going to a Funeral, we could all Wear Black Robes, just to Remind us of that Long Lonesome Dark Night, when we will have to Walk that Lonesome Valley of the Shadow of Death all by ourselves, even if the Tombs are made of Colorful Polished Marbles. ‡

U-[_] University Students should have to Wear Pink Robes with Red Trimmings, just to make them look Sexier: beCause they need to get Married. †§‡

V-[_] You must be a Victim of Capitalism. University Students should Wear Solid Colors of Clothing with Polka Dots of Various Colors, according as each School Wants them — such as Yellow Robes with Red Polka Dots: beCause no such Universities will be Needed, now that we have the Internet to Learn from, which will have Free University Classes concerning any given Subjects. However, if it is something that cannot be Learned on the Internet, it can be Learned in Home-craft Workshops. For Example, the Medical Doctor who Resets Broken Bones can do it in his Home-craft Workshop: beCause that is his Craft, who may also have his Nurses, Midwives, and whomever surrounding him in the Swanky Palace or Swanky Castle Hospital, who could all be Dressed in Pink Clothing with Dark Pink Trimmings. †§‡

W-[_] Warriors should be Dressed in Scarlet Robes with Bright Yellow Stripes down their Backs: beCause of being Spiritual Cowards, who are Afraid to take up their Swords of Truths to Defeat their Enemies. †§‡

X-[_] X-amount of People will Want their Traditional Clothing, which they may have, and Wear whenever they are not Working as Working Soldiers. ‡

Y-[_] You might have gotten by with such Nonsense, 4 or 5 Centuries Ago, during Yesteryears; but, these are Modern Times, when People are Free to Choose whatever Capitalist Clothing might be Found for Sale, which is a BIG Business with the Changes in Seasons. Therefore, if the People Accept the Uniformity Nonsense, Capitalism will DIE! †§‡

Z-[_] The Zeal of **The Worldwide People's Revolution!®** will Kill Capitalism. Please Check with an X the Following Boxes for your Favorite Colors:

A List of FAIR Swanky Wages!

    01-[_] White; 02-[_] Blue; 03-[_] Yellow; 04-[_] Green; 05-[_] Gray; 06-[_] Brown; 07-[_] Black; 08-[_] Red; 09-[_] Orange; 10-[_] Pink; 11-[_] Scarlet; 12-[_] Purple; 13-[_] Violet; 14-[_] Maroon (Chestnut); 15-[_] Gold; 16-[_] Silver; 17-[_] Turquoise; 18-[_] Emerald; 19-[_] Sapphire; 20-[_] Blood; 21-[_] Skin; 22-[_] Red Cedar; 23-[_] Mahogany; 24-[_] Black Walnut; 25-Rosewood; 26-[_] Pine; 27-[_] Ask; 28-[_] Redwood; 29-[_] Hickory; 30-[_] Other (please Name it) ...

08-07 [_] Extremely Difficult Skilled Work — such as Lifting Rocks that Weigh more than 100 Pounds, or Timbers of equal Weight — should receive Maximum Swanky Wages, if such Work is Constant and Requires Special Skills. Therefore, that Labor would be worth 100$ per Hour, plus Incentive Pay for Heat or Cold and/or Danger. Such Work would only be Appropriate for Strong Men, and only for 4 Hours per Day. However, if someone Wanted more Work, that Person could do Common Labor, or Easy Labor, so as to not Overwork himself, and thus Contract Physical Ailments — such as a Bad Back, which can also be Obtained by not knowing HOW to Work Correctly: so as to not Hurt the Back. We will try to Limit all such Work, and let Machines take care of Heavy Rocks and Timbers, if it is Practical. Most Heavy Objects can be Handled with Ease by having more Men Handle them with the Correct Tools, whereby it would be called Hard Labor or just Common Skilled Labor. Hard Unskilled Labor is worth 80$ per Hour, and Difficult Skilled Labor is worth 90$ per Hour, plus Incentive Pay for Extreme Weather and Danger.

08-08 [_] So, O Elected King, it Appears that you have Divided Labor into 10 Categories, which are as follows:

    01-[_] Super Easy Unskilled Labor — 10$ per Hour — such a Guard Duty.

    02-[_] Super Easy Skilled Labor — 20$ per Hour — such as the Labor of Babysitting.

    03-[_] Easy Unskilled Labor — 30$ per Hour — such as Watering Gardens and Trees.

    04-[_] Easy Skilled Labor — 40$ per Hour — such as the Labor of Authors, Secretaries, Preachers, Politicians, Scientists, Inventors, Teachers, Professors, Judges and Lawyers.

    05-[_] Common Unskilled Labor — 50$ per Hour — such as Hoeing Weeds in a Garden, Cleaning House, Washing Dishes, and Picking Fruits.

    06-[_] Common Skilled Labor — 60$ per Hour — such as Setting Tiles on Walls, Laying Bricks, Making Boots, Sewing Clothing, and Wrapping Meat.

    07-[_] Hard Unskilled Labor — 70$ per Hour — such as Shoveling Sand or Gravel continuously. (The Size of the Shovel could Change the Value of the Labor. Small People should use Smaller Shovels. Large People should use Larger Shovels, just to be Fair about it.)

(The Equitable Wage System!)

08-[_] Hard Skilled Labor — 80$ per Hour — such as Laying Stones on a Wall that weigh 50 to 100 Pounds each. (The Mortar Mixing would be Common Skilled Labor, which someone else would do for the Stonemason, so as to keep him Busy with his Skill.)

09-[_] Extremely Difficult Unskilled Labor — 90$ per Hour — such as Lifting Rocks or Timbers that weight 100 pounds or more, continuously, plus 10$ Incentive Pay for the Danger of it, for covering the Cost of Insurance, plus 10$ for Extreme Weather.

10-[_] Extremely Difficult Skilled Labor — 100$ per Hour — such as Laying those Heavy Cut Stones or Rough Rocks on a Wall, after they are Washed Properly. (Do not Skimp on the Cement in the Mortar; but, use Extra Cement, and Fresh Cement, which is made and used during the same Day: so that such Stonework will Endure for thousands of Years.)

08-09 [_] Well, there are a million or more Different Kinds of Labor and Special Skills; but, generally-speaking, those 10 Categories will Cover most Kinds of Labor, even though there could be "Endless" Arguments about the "Fair" Pay: beCause of Jumping from 10$ to 20$, for Example, when there might only be 2 or 3 dollars-worth of Difference. And then there are the "Eternal" Arguments about WHO did the Most Work. For Example, if a Person is Shoveling Sand Rapidly or Slowly, he can move 2 Tons or 1 Ton in one Hour, roughly-speaking. No one is going to Measure what Work gets done: because of not wanting to Waste Time; but, it is Obvious when someone is Working Hard or Soft. I once had an Interesting Experience with a certain Citiot, whom I gave a Pick and Shovel to, and asked him to Dig a Hole for Planting a Tree, many Years ago, while I went to do something else, and came back 4 Hours later, to Discover that the Hole was only 6 inches deep and a foot wide, when I asked him to make it 2 feet deep and 4 feet wide. It was not hard Ground, nor Difficult Digging; but, he had no Idea what one foot was, let along 4 feet. Perhaps he thought it was the width of his Big Toe. At any rate, it became Obvious that he had never done any Manual Labor during his entire Life; but, he still liked to Eat. I am Sure that he would have Starved to Death without some Welfare Aid from someone.

08-10 [_] So, O Elected King, it looks like we would have to Draft all such People into the Seventh Swanky Army of Working Soldiers, and send them through Basic Training, whereby they might Learn HOW to Dig Holes, Drive Nails, Cut Boards, Bolt Things Together, and Wash their Hands after using the Toilet, huh?

08-11 [_] Well, some People are not Willing to Learn anything, even if they were Drafted into some Army of Working Soldiers, with the Option to Volunteer to Join some other Army with TWICE the Pay: beCause they are Physically and perhaps Mentally SICK. Therefore, the First Line of Action would be to Remove the Poisons from their Bowels, which might Require a Week or 2 of Fasting, and a couple Bottles of Prune Juice, Grape Juice, Fresh Orange Juice, and whatever is Needed for FLUSHING OUT those Poisons, whereby their Attitudes would be Transformed. And then, when they get Hungry, show to them a Luscious Garden with all Kinds of Vegetables to Eat, whereby they might Discover the Real World, and WHERE Foods come from, including Chickens, if that is what they Want to Eat, which they can Butcher, Cook, and Eat, just for the Experience of it, which is called the Higher School of Superior Learning. †§‡

08-12 [_] O Elected King, such a Drafted Working Soldier is likely to come after your own Head with an Ax in his Hand, which would otherwise be used for Removing the Head of the Chicken: beCause he would just Naturally HATE you for Drafting him: beCause of not Wanting to WORK for a Living, even if you are only asking for 4 Hours of his Services per Day. After all, X-amount of Young People are SPOILED ROTTEN, nowadays! †§‡

08-13 [_] Well, I Agree that some of them are Spoiled to some Degree; but, when they See what Great Things those Voluntary Working Soldiers have Accomplished, they will also no doubt get Inspired to Join them. But, if not, we can put them to Work on Building Railways, Digging Out Tunnels, and Handling Rocks in Rock Quarries, until they come to their Right Senses: because there is no Need for Rebellion against the Economic System that I Propose. After all, they may Choose to do the Easiest Work there is, if they Hate Hard Work that much. Otherwise, if they do not Cooperate with us, they might get Drafted into some Army of Murderous Soldiers, whereby they will have no Options to Choose from, and will either Learn to MOVE QUICKLY, or get Killed! Indeed, that is WHY God Allows all such Wars: so that we might Learn how much Better it is to Learn to Cooperate with each other, and to Build those **"GLORIOUS Swanky Hotels Castles and Fortresses,"** which will make Wars Obsolete: beCause it is Impossible to Conquer such a Fortress from the Outside: beCause they are Designed for Defense. However, no Lazy People could ever Build such a Fortress. †§‡

08-14 [_] O Elected King, why not just Forget about those People who do not Voluntarily Join **"The Swanky Associations of Working Soldiers!"** — as in, let them go to Hell? After all, when X-amount of Fortresses get Finished, those Cities of Confusion will be Abandoned, and only the Lowest Scumbags, Thieves, Liars, Robbers, Murderers, Drug Addicts, and Red Jew Criminals will be left in them: beCause the Righteous People will Abandon them. Therefore, they will Destroy themselves, while the Righteous People will be Safe and Prosperous. ‡

08-15 [_] Well, it would be Okay with me if they all just Starved to Death, if they were Unwilling to Learn and Work. However, the "Equal Rights" People would be Upset, and would be Protesting against **"The New RIGHTEOUS One-World Government,"** saying that it is their DUTY to make Sure that no one Starves to Death. Therefore, we will likely have to have a DRAFT for the "Incorrigibles," just to Save them from themselves, who may have to be run through a Swanky Institution of Correction, whereby the Meanness will be Worked Out of them. After all, we are not Asking them to Sacrifice any Good Thing to Join Forces with us; nor are we Asking them to Say nor Do any Evil Thing. However, if you Disagree, please Speak Up!

(The Equitable Wage System!)

— Chapter 09 —

Arguments Against Fair Swanky Wages!

09-01 [_] O Elected King, I Object to your Insane Wages, which are NOT at all FAIR: beCause everyone Knows for a Fact that those Chinese and Mexicans are Harder Workers than Americans and Germans, who would be getting RICH, just by their Labors, alone! Moreover, the Market would be FLOODED with far too much Money, which is called INFLATION, whereby it would Require no less than a Boxcar full of Money, just to Buy a Wooden / Plastic House and a Car. †§

09-02 [_] You must have had your Eyes Closed while you were Pretending to read the previous Chapters. WHY would anyone Want to Buy a Wooden / Plastic Firetrap Mouse-infested Cockroach Den, when they could be Living in a Beautiful Multi-million-dollar Swanky Stone Dome Home Complex? Moreover, what makes you Vainly Imagine that Americans and Germans are not Able and Willing to Work Equally as hard as Chinese and Mexicans? Indeed, few People on the Earth are as Hardworking as Germans and Americans, most of whom are Germans, or at least Europeans, who are all Hardworking People.

09-03 [_] O Elected King, if I could not OWN such a House and Complex, I would not Want to Live in it: beCause it would not be MY House.

09-04 [_] Well, does the President of the United States OWN the White House, in Washington, in the District of Corruption? Of course not! Neither do tens of millions of People OWN the Houses that they Live in, and it does not make them Despised in the Eyes of God, who said: *"The Land is MY Land,"* which Means that it Belongs to GOD. (See *Second Chronicles 7:20; Isaiah 14:25; Jeremiah 2:7; 16:18; Ezekiel 38:16; Joel 3:2; and* **Leviticus 25:23—24,** *KJV.*)

09-05 [_] So, are you saying, O King, that People should not be Seeking to OWN anything: beCause it will only PUFF UP their Pride, whereby they will be Deceived by their Possessions?

09-06 [_] Well, when you do not Own the Swanky Palace that you Live in, it does Help to keep you more Humble and Honest. Therefore, it is much less Deceiving: beCause it is Difficult, if not Impossible, to be very Proud of the Place that you do not "Own." Indeed, it Helps to Keep a Person in Tune with God, who must be the Owner. However, in our Case, **"The New RIGHTEOUS One-World Government"** would be the Owner, which Means that it would not Belong to any one Person; but, it would Belong to **"The Swanky Associations of Working Soldiers,"** who did the Hard Work to Build those **"GLORIOUS Swanky Hotels Castles and Fortresses!"** (Beautiful Planned City States for WISE Intelligent Well-Educated People with Common Sense and Good Understanding!) By The Worldwide People's Revolution!®

09-07 [_] So, O Elected King, if no one Owned their own House, Workshop, Cisterns, and Garden, what Need would there be for Wages, much less for Swanky Wages, seeing that any Hungry Person could simply go to their Garden and get whatever they might Want to Eat, or else get their Food from their Walk-in Cooler / Root Cellar / Freezer / or Pantry; or otherwise, Visit their Royal Swanky Buffet, and Eat all they Want, for FREE? Indeed, if each Person did his or her 4 Hours of Common Labor per Day, he or she could get a Free Ticket for Eating, while Visitors would have to Pay for their Foods, unless they were also Members of **"The Swanky Associations of Working Soldiers!" (A Fascinating Collection of Various Kinds of Voluntary Working Soldiers!) By The Worldwide People's Revolution!®** Book 018. So, HOW would those Visitors Obtain the necessary Money for Buying such Foods, seeing that Counterfeit American Money would not be Legal in any such Fortresses: beCause it was not Earned by Honest Labor when it was Printed?

09-08 [_] Well, those Visitors would have to do some Work, before Eating, or else Exchange some Valuable Thing for their Foods, since their Counterfeit Money would be no Good. So, that would get a bit Complicated: beCause of being a Barter System. However, if they did have something Valuable to Trade for Swanky Money, they could do that, and then use that Money for whatever they Want. However, I am Sure that most of them would not Like the High Prices of the Foods and Drinks at Swanky Fortresses: beCause those Prices would be Based on Swanky Wages. For Example, if a Fruit Picker is Earning 50$ per Hour for Picking Apples, and Harvests 4 Bushels per Hour, those Apples must Sell for enough Money to Pay for his Work — Planting the Tree, Pruning the Tree, Watering the Tree, Feeding the Tree Compost, Making the Compost, Moving the Compost, and Picking the Fruits, which might Amount to 100$ for just one Bushel of Apples — Depending on how Successfully he Managed it all. Some Apple Trees do not Bear Apples for 6 Years, and even if they do, the Trees are not supposed to be Allowed to Produce any Fruits: beCause it Weakens the Tree, which is True for almost all Fruit Trees, Nut Trees, Grape Vines, and Berry Bushes. In other Words, when those Trees Bear some Fruits, it is Best to Pluck them Off as soon as they Appear: so that the Trees are not Weakened by Bearing Fruits when they are too Young. In other Words, those Fruits should be Aborted. ‡

09-09 [_] So, O Elected King, the Price of those first Harvested Apples would have to Cover the Costs of 6 Years of Husbandry, or Caring for the Trees, huh?

09-10 [_] Well, that seems to be Reasonable enough, except that few People would be Willing to Pay such High Prices for those First Fruits, which might be 100$ each, if there were only a few of them. However, there might be other Cheaper Fruits at the Royal Buffet — such as Blackberries, which Produce well within 3 Years; and Blueberries, which Produce well within 5 Years. Therefore, the Abundance of Fruits at the Royal Swanky Buffet would Depend on how Old the Fortress is, and how Well the Plants were taken Care of. Hopefully, within 6 Years, everything will be "Pumping," as they say, and everyone will be Free to Eat all that they might Want from their own Gardens, Vineyards, and Orchards. Therefore, it does Require much Patience at the Beginning of such an Operation. In Fact, we might have to be Contented with Watermelons, Cantaloupes, Cucumbers, Squashes, Potatoes, Kale, Green Onions, and whatever Survival Foods that we can Grow, until the Fortresses get Built. After all, I saw a single Apple for 1$, not long ago, which were 50 Cents per Bushel when I was a Boy. Therefore, Inflation is already a Major Problem, which will be Reduced more and more, as we Build those Swanky Fortresses: beCause of the Fruit Trees Bearing more and more Fruits. Meanwhile, **"The Swanky Associations of Fruit Pickers"** will have to Harvest Fruits from whatever Trees are now Planted, in spite of being Sprayed with Harmful Poisons, if they are Wanting Fruits to Eat.

(The Equitable Wage System!)

09-11 [_] O King, Chances are that almost no one in the World will be Interested in Building any Swanky Fortresses, until at least one of them gets Finished, whereby they can See what such Beautiful Planned City States are like. Therefore, if I were you, I would not be getting my Hopes Built Up too High. After all, this is a Visionless Generation, you know. †

09-12 [_] Well, those Evening News Reports about Wild Fires, Floods, Tornadoes, Hurricanes, Mudslides, Droughts, Famines, Earthquakes, Tsunamis, and other Natural Disasters, will Help to give to them some Vision and Foresight — and especially if they are the Victims of such Disasters. Otherwise, it is a Hopeless Case, I would say, which can all be Blamed onto those Lying Red Jews, who Control the News Media, Movies, Book Publishing Companies, Magazine Operations, and Newspapers, who could use their Freedom of Speech to WARN the Masses of People, and to Direct them toward my Inspired Books, which have Guaranteed Solutions. ‡

09-13 [_] O Elected King, it always seems like the People who most Need the Necessary Money for doing Good Things, are always Restricted by their Poverty. For Example, if you had the Billions of Dollars that have been Wasted on Election Deceptions, you could easily put a Copy of this Book into every Mailbox in the Country, whereby the Masses of People might Learn about your Master Plan. Therefore, it must not be the Will of God that they should Learn about it. After all, God supposedly Owns all of the Land in the World, which he could Sell for getting enough Money to Publish your Books, Properly. †§‡§§

09-14 [_] Well, you just have to Remember that Satan is in Charge of this World of Woes; and therefore, there is not much that Righteous People can Do, except to Fast and Pray for God to Intervene; and he might not be Interested in it: beCause of not being Ready to put Chains on Satan, and Cast him into that Bottomless Pit that *the Book of Revelation* speaks of. Whatever the Case, it is up to us Human Beings to Change the Situation, or else Suffer with the Consequences of Climate Changes, Melting Icebergs, Rising Sea Levels, Severe Storms, Earthquakes, Famines, Extinctions of Animals, the Destruction of the Coral Reefs, the Pollutions of Air, Waters, and Lands, the Unemployment Problems, the Deadly Nuclear Power ElecTrickery Plant Meltdowns, and whatever might come: beCause of the EVILS of Capitalism, which most Capitalists are not Willing to Confess. Meanwhile, my Readers should take up the Cause, and do their Best to Spread the Words. ‡

09-15 [_] O Elected King, there are probably a thousand and one Unanswered Questions about your Swanky Wages, which you have Carefully Avoided: beCause, if you had your Way, all Money would be done away with, and everyone would simply go to Work to Construct those **"GLORIOUS Swanky Hotels Castles and Fortresses,"** which would make it Possible for almost everyone to become Moderately Rich. After all, there is a Great DEMAND for it. Indeed, all Debts could be Forgiven, as Moses wrote, and we could Declare Liberty throughout all of the Land, unto all of the People, and thus be Rid of those Lying Red Jews, who have Drug us into this Bottomless Pit of Confusion and Debts. (See *Leviticus 25.*)

— Chapter 10 —

The Confusion of Dealing with Money

10-01 [_] Of all of the Systems in this World of Wonders, the Monetary Systems are most Complicated and Confusing. For Example, using the FAIR Swanky Wages System, a certain Working Soldier could Work for 2.5 Hours early during the Morning, when it is Cool and Comfortable for Extremely Difficult Skilled Labor; and then he could Work during the Afternoon for 3 Hours of Easy Unskilled Labor, and one Hour of Common Skilled Labor before Retiring for the Day. Therefore, how much Pay should he Receive for that Day's Work? Well, the 2.5 Hours would be Worth 250$, plus 90$ for the Easy Unskilled Labor, plus 60$ for the one Hour of Common Skilled Labor, for a Total of 400$, minus 4 Hours of Common Unskilled Labor Wages for his Privilege of Living within a Swanky Fortress, equals 200$. Indeed, he must Contribute 4 Hours of Common Unskilled Labor, per Day, 6 Days per Week, or the Equivalent thereof, in Exchange for Living in a Swanky Fortress, which Amounts to 24 Hours per Week, times 50$ per Hour, equals 1,200$ per Week, or 4,800$ per Month: beCause there are Exactly 28 Days, or 4 Weeks in every Month, according to my New Calendar, which you can Study in: **"For the Love of Money!"** Book 003. Therefore, if a Voluntary Working Soldier does an Average of 24 Hours of Common Unskilled Labor per Week, all of his or her Needs will be Supplied, including Housing, Electricity, Foods, Drinks, Clothing, Water for the Garden, Transportation, Entertainments, and everything that he or she might Need: beCause of Joining **"The Swanky Associations of Working Soldiers!"** Book 018. Indeed, no Money will be Needed for Obtaining those Things: beCause it is just a matter of Exchanging Work for Living in the Fortress. Therefore, each Person will be Earning "CREDITS" for his or her Labor, which will be Credited to his or her Living Expenses. However, everyone will be Welcome to do more Work for Earning Swanky Wages, if they Want to, whereby they can Save Money or Credit for Buying Personal Property, if they Want it — such as Special Computers, Special Telephones, Special Furniture, Special Books, or even Special Clothing, even though all of those Things will be Provided Free of Charge at the Fortress. However, a Person might Want something that he or she Believes is a "Better Quality Product." If so, they will be Free to Buy those Things, and it will not Bother me nor you. However, all of the Tools, Furniture, and other Things that are Produced by **"The Swanky Associations of Working Soldiers"** will be Top Quality Swanky Products, if I have my Way, including Diamond-studded Rolex Watches for everyone within the System, which will Require some Time to get them Made; but, I would say that within 10 to 12 Years, it is Possible. Moreover, many Trees for Special Lumber will have to be Planted, which will Require a hundred Years or more to Grow Up, whereby Special Hand-crafted Furniture can be made from it, during the Future: beCause there is no Way to Speed Up that Process. However, in the Meantime, Fine Hand-crafted Furniture can be made from Poplars, Pines, Firs, and Fast-growing Trees, which can be Beautiful, even if it is not as Beautiful as Mahogany, White Oak, Rosewood, Red Cedar, or some Exotic Wood. Indeed, Capitalism has already Ruined the Chances of having such Fine Furniture during our Lifetimes; and many Special Trees are now Extinct — Thanks to Capitalism. Therefore, we will just have to be Patient, until we are Born Again into this World, which will Hopefully be Greatly Improved by that Time — that is, unless God Judges us to not be Worthy to be Born Again into this World, whereby he may Send our

(The Equitable Wage System!)

Spirits to some other Lower Order of Worlds, where there are even less Materials to Work with — such as the Interior of Mars, which may only have a Limited Amount of Good Things in abundance! For Example, it may have lots of Sand, Gravel, and Limestone; but, no Marbles, no Granites, no Onyx, no Gemstones, no Silver, no Gold, no Oil, no Gas, and no Sunrises nor Sunsets, much less any Stars to Study: because of Inhabiting the INSIDE of Mars, only, which would be like a Prison Camp, you might say, which would have its Limitations on almost everything, including Foods. Indeed, there might only be a few Things to even Eat: beCause of not having the Great Diversity of Foods that we have in this World of Wonders, whereby their are Countless Combinations of Foods and Drinks. ‡

10-02 [_] O Elected King, you Surely do not Believe in Reincarnation, do you?

10-03 [_] I Surely Hope to God that I do Believe in Reincarnation: beCause, if this Life is the END of Life for me, that would be Extremely Depressing! Nevertheless, I Realize that some False Religions do Teach all such Outlandish LIES, in spite of reading what Jesus said: *"And whosoever shall speak a word against the Son of man, it shall be forgiven him; but whosoever shall speak against the Holy Spirit, it shall not be forgiven him, neither in **this world, nor in that which is to come.**" — Matthew 12:32, American Standard Version (ASV),* which is clearly stating that there is **a World to Come** when a Person can be Forgiven; but, NOT if such a Person has Spoken against the Holy Spirit, who Inspired Chapter 03, Verses 07—12, which you should read at least once again.

10-04 [_] O Elected King, I must Confess that your Beliefs are Superior to mine: beCause they make more Overall Sense — including the Elimination of all Money, which is not Needed for True Prosperity, which the Mayan Indians Lived Well without, for Example, and there were no Poor People among them when Hernando Cortez Discovered them. †‡

10-05 [_] Well, Cortez Discovered and Conquered the Aztecs, not the Mayan Indians. Nevertheless, it is probably True that the Mayan Indians had a Superior Society, as did the Aztecs, who certainly had no Poor People among them, nor any Greedy Selfish Rich People, even though there was an Upper Class and a Lower Class of People, whom I call Masters and Servants, which is the Perfect Form of Good Government, just as long as the Upper Class is Paid LESS for their Services than the Lower Class, who should all be Paid According to the DIFFICULTY of their WORK. For Example, it is not at all Difficult for me to Write my Inspired Books: beCause I only have to Listen to the Holy Spirit, and Type on my Keyboard! However, for a Politician to Write a Speech, it might be most Difficult, or even Mentally Painful, whereby all such Speeches are Revised a dozen or more Times before they are Acceptable to them, which is WHY they often Hire Speech Writers to do it for them, as was the Case for almost all Presidents except for George Washington, Thomas Jefferson, John Adams, John Quincy Adams, Andrew Jackson, Abraham Lincoln, Theodore Roosevelt, Woodrow Wilson, Franklin Roosevelt, Harry Truman, John F. Kennedy, Lyndon B. Johnson, Jimmy Carter, and Barrack Obama. †‡

10-06 [_] O Elected King, you will do Well to take Counsel with a Professional Economist before you Publish this Uninspired Book: beCause any Economic Child could Blow you Out of the Water, as they say, and without any Bombs! First of all, you have not yet Established any Righteous One-World Government, much less Obtained all of the Land, Mountains of Rocks, Mineral Rights, Water Rights, and everything that would be Necessary for Building so much as

ONE of those Not-so-Glorious Swanky Disasters, which no one would Want to Live in, except you and your Crazy Brother Vern, who have no Idea what you are Talking about: beCause it is Impossible to Build a Moat that is 100 Miles Long: beCause the Earth just Naturally SHIFTS, and sometimes it Shifts every Month or so, and especially wherever those Ignorant Fools have been Fracking the Earth for Oil, which have Caused Earthquakes in Various Places. Therefore, Knowing for a Fact that the Land SHIFTS itself around, and maybe 3 to 6 inches at a Time, there is no Way to Build any such LONG Moats, which would soon be Leaking Water Out of Countless CRACKS! So, what does your Holy Spirit have to say about that, your Highness? †§‡

10-07 [_] Well, have you not Heard that, *"Wherever there is a Will, there is a Way"*? First of all, all Swanky Fortresses should be Built on BEDROCKS, which are much more Stable than normal Grounds, even if we must Dig Down DEEP into the Earth to Discover those Bedrocks, which will Require HUGE Swanky LAND-MOVING Machines, which will Remove all of the Trees, Topsoil, Gravel, Sand, Subsoil, and Clay, while Separating all of those Building Materials for Use, later on, until that Machine gets down to Bedrock; and then the Swanky Cisterns will be Built on that Bedrock, until there is a Good Foundation for the Moat to be Built on TOP of those Large Cisterns, which will Support the entire Swanky Fortress, which will have Millions of Large Swanky Cisterns under it for Water Storage, which will all be Lined with Ceramic Tiles on Solid Concrete Cylindrical Walls, about 60 feet in Diameter; and then each Cylinder will be Capped with a Solid Concrete Dome, which will be Level on the Top, and about 10 feet THICK in the Center of the True Dome. Therefore, the Moat will not be Slipping around nor Cracking: beCause it will all be SOLID. Moreover, once we Begin to Pour the Special Swanky Concrete for the Moat, going in both Directions at the same Time, we will not Stop Pouring Concrete, until the far Ends are Joined, Head to Head, and about 20 feet THICK, being made of Concrete and LARGE Rough Clean ROCKS, even as big as Cars and Trucks, whereby the Concrete will Act as Mortar between the Rough Rocks, which have to be Vibrated by Overhanging Cranes. And thus, like "Magic," the Manmade Foundation for the Moat will be Ready for Soaking it under Cool Water the very next Day. Yes, the Architects and Engineers will Figure Out HOW to do all of that: so as to have a GOOD Swanky Moat that is 1,000 feet Wide and 200 feet Deep, when it is Finished: beCause of making the Sloped Walls for the Moat one Layer at a Time, about 10 feet Deep, using those same Rough Rocks and Swanky Concrete, which is made from Fresh Cement, which is Used Immediately, even before it Cools Off: beCause ICE Water is Added to the Mixture of Concrete, in order to Prevent it from Overheating. Moreover, that Work will have to be done during Cold Weather, when the Conditions are just Riit: beCause it would be a Disaster if it came a Pouring Rain during the Operation, and thus Ruined the Concrete. †‡

> A-[_] I am an Architect, and I Agree — there is a Possibility of it Working, if such a Solid Bedrock can be Found; but, do not Ask me WHERE it is Located: beCause I have no Idea, and I am not Sure that anyone else has any Idea. After all, a 100-mile-wide Swanky Fortress is a HUGE Building Project, which would Require MILLIONS of Working Soldiers to get it Finished in less than 100 Years! †§‡

> B-[_] No such Building will ever be Built: beCause of LOGISTICS! Indeed, getting all of those HUGE Boulders Lined Up and Ready to Use would be a MASSIVE PROBLEM, among many other Problems — such as Mixing no less than a TRILLION Tons of Concrete within just one Week! Moreover, there is the HOLE in the Ground to Deal with, which is likely to fill up with Rainwater or Seepage before anything can Begin! ‡

(The Equitable Wage System!)

C-[_] I Confess that it would be more Exciting than going to the Moon with a Canoe attached to the Lunar Landing Module, in order to go Fishing with Joseph Smith Junior, who Sincerely Believed (as did Sir Isaac Newton) that there are little Green Men Living INSIDE of the Moon, if you can Believe it, O Elected King! {See www.Amazon.com for: **"The New MAGNIFIED Version of The Book of MOORMUN!" (The Story of the White and Dark Indians in the Americas!) By The Worldwide People's Revolution!®**, Book 040, which comes in 2 Volumes. Be Sure to begin with Volume 1.}

D-[_] Damn it! — not even Poor Old Miserable Uncle Sam could Accomplish such a Great Feat: beCause there are NO Swanky Land-moving Machines on the Earth, nor can anyone make one without Melting Down all of the Army Tanks in the World, just to get enough Steel for making it, which would also Require Engines / Motors, no less than 100 Times the Size of the Biggest Bulldozers, as in D575A-3's. After all, we are talking about Moving a MOUNTAIN of Dirt and Rocks within a Week or 2, and 400 Miles Long, just to make a Swanky MOAT around a Swanky Fortress: so that some Old Man can go Fishing in it, Swimming in it, Ice-skating on it, or Canoeing in it! Why not make Short Water Tanks 200 feet long and 100 feet wide and 50 feet deep, and Join them Ass to Ass around the Fortress, if any such Moats are Needed for Keeping Out Terrorists? Indeed, each little Moat could have Fishes Stocked in it of Various Kinds of Fishes, Snakes, and Aljeegaaterz. †§‡ {See www.Amazon.com for: **"Terrorists Beware that your Days are Numbered!" (HOW to Bring those Terrorist Attacks to a Screeching HALT!)**, Book 043, plus: **"The UGLY Scarred Dishonest Face of Poor Old Miserable UNCLE SAM!" (A Memorial Day Legacy!) By The Worldwide People's Revolution!®** Book 054.}

E-[_] Educated People know that it is Impossible to make such Large Moats: beCause the Earth is forever Shifting around, which might Shift by 3 or 4 inches within just one Mile, which would Crack the Moat, and Cause it to LEAK, which would Ruin the entire Swankless Project. †§‡

F-[_] I Fail to Understand WHY we do not just Build Short Moats or Large Tanks for holding Fishes, if the Idea is to have some Place to go Fishing?

G-[_] God Knows that all such Moats would become Giant Mosquito Hatcheries for the Zika Virus Mosquitoes: beCause Water must be MOVING, in order to Prevent it.

H-[_] HUMBUG! God Knows that the whole Idea is INSANE: beCause no such Moats are Needed for Keeping OUT those Wicked ISIS (Israeli Secret Instigation Services) Terrorists, who are the Meanest of Computer Hackers, who should be Boiled in HOT Used Motor Oil! Moreover, the sooner, the Better. †§‡

I-[_] I am an Innocent Lamb of God; and I cannot Understand WHY we cannot have Running Fresh Clean Living Water in all of the Swanky Moats, by Means of Hydroelectric Power whenever the Wind is not Blowing. However, when the Wind is Blowing, we can use Giant Swanky PUMPS for Creating an Artistic Swanky Waterfalls at the Head of the Moat, which causes the Water to Run all of the Way around the Swanky Fortress, and back to the Waterfalls, where it is Pumped back Up to the Top of the Waterfalls, whereby all of the Water in the Moat would be continually Circulating around the Fortress, which would be Perfect for those Freshwater Fishes, and for Innocent Lambs and Kids to go Fishing. Indeed, the Moat could have a Gentle Slope from the Waterfalls all of the way around the Fortress, by dropping 2 inches every 100 feet, or a Total of 1,689.6 inches in 16 Miles of the Moat, which is a Drop of only 140 feet. Therefore, if the Swanky Water Pumps could Pump a Million Gallons of Water per Minute, it would keep the Water Flowing around the Fortress, if the Moat were 1,000 feet Wide and 200 feet Deep, which is most Practical for those Freshwater Fishes, who would be Breeding inside of their little Manmade Stone Dome Home Complexes within the Sides of the Moat, which would have Windows at the Ends of Tunnels for Visitors and Tourists to View the Fishes from Outside of the Moat, under the Swanky Fortresses, which would be Designed for that in Mind. After all, there are Multitudes of Fishes that would Love it, while People would get to Enjoy Eating some of them, whereby they would get their Necessary Proteins, and thus be Healthier and Happier for it, even though that can be Disputed in a Courtroom. †§‡

J-[_] Justice Demands that no Mosquitoes are Hatched Out anywhere around a Swanky Fortress: beCause we do not Want nor Need Malaria and other Sicknesses, which were Obviously Created by that Hebrew God, who should be brought to Court, and Charged with Murder for all of the Millions of Innocent Children who have Died with Malaria and other Horrible Diseases, and especially that Disease that Inflicts the Minds of those Red Jew Computer Hackers. †§‡

K-[_] King Jesus will take Good Care of them when he Returns with Devouring FIRE at his Command. Yes, they will either Repent, or Perish! ‡

L-[_] Lots of Laughs! King Jesus is far too Gentle and Merciful. He is likely to Reward them with **"Beautiful Swanky PALACES!"** After all, he had some of that same Blood in himself, being a Son of Joseph, who was of the Tribe of Judah, while his Mother was of the Tribe of Levi. Therefore, it is Understandable WHY he would also Love Money more than God, even more than All that is GOOD. †§‡

M-[_] It is Time to give those Lying Zionist Red Jews the MONTEZUMA TREATMENT, whereby we would have to Haul Out their Millions of Tons of Gold Bricks, and make some of them Molten Hot, and pour the Molten Gold down their Greedy Throats! Yes, that might Inspire their Children to Think Twice before Establishing another Needless Red Jew Banking System, as Moses might say, who never had any such Banking System for the next 2,000 Years; and the Israelites Prospered without them, even as all Nations did, until the Time of Christ. †§‡

N-[_] Not everyone is so Selfish and Greedy as those Lying Red Jews; but, whomever is that Selfish and Greedy does not Deserve to Live in any Swanky Palace. Indeed, all such Niggers should be Born in Mars.

O-[_] In my Honest Opinion, and most likely in the Honest Opinions of most People, it would Require as much Gasoline to make all of that Concrete for the Base of that one Swanky Fortress, as Americans might Burn Up in their Cars during one Week, which

(The Equitable Wage System!)

would be Horrible! I Mean that it would Require that much Gas for making the Cement for the Concrete, which must be Thoroughly Baked Limestone. Therefore, it would be a HUGE Waste of Gasoline to Build such Fortresses. †§‡ {See www.Amazon.com for: **"The Environmentalists' Paradise!" (HOW almost Everyone could be Living in a Beautiful Manmade Paradise!) By The Worldwide People's Revolution!®** Book 035.}

P-[_] I Hope to God that most People are not as Irrational as you are. Indeed, if that is all of the Energy that is Required for Building 64 million Swanky Cisterns on 10,000 square Miles of Land, I would say that it is Extremely Cheap. After all, just one Cistern would have no less than 2,000 Tons of Concrete and Rocks in it, before the Dome or Cap is put over it, which might be another 500 Tons of Rocks and Concrete. Therefore, if it Requires six 90-pound Bags of Cement per Ton of Concrete, not including the Rough Rocks, that would be no less than 15,000 Bags of Cement, just for one Cistern that holds a million Gallons of Water, times 64 million, equals about 960,000,000,000 Bags of Cement for all of those Cisterns. However, by Building Cisterns like a Honeycomb, in Hexagons, much Concrete can be Saved for other Projects: because of not needing so many Walls, even though the Walls would be Weaker than Cylindrical Walls. However, if those Hexagon Walls are thick enough, they will work fine. All of those Cisterns could be Joined by simply having Open Doorways for the Water to run from one Cistern into another one, whereby the Water Table would be Exactly the same in all of the Cisterns at the same Time, for 4 Miles, or 400 Miles, and in all Directions, which Water Table could be Used Wisely for Leveling all Parts of the Swanky Fortress. Therefore, the Water could be Measured in just one Cistern, in order to Discover Exactly how much Water is in Storage, and whether or not those Cisterns could "Absorb" any Pouring Rains. However, getting them Cleaned, now and then, would be a Major Problem, without Entrances to them from Above. †‡

      01-[_] I Object, your Honor: beCause, if those Cisterns are not Independent from one another, some Terrorist might manage to Poison all of the Waters within all of those Cisterns at the same Time. †‡

      02-[_] Such a Terrorist should be run through a Swanky Meat Grinder when he is Discovered. †

      03-[_] Suppose he is not Discovered?

      04-[_] Suppose he is Discover, and also ran through a Meat Grinder — HOW will that Remedy the Problems that will be Created by Poisoning the Water, which would Amount to TRILLIONS of Gallons of Water, if there are 64 Million Cisterns with a Million Gallons, each?

      05-[_] It actually equals 64,000,000,000,000 Gallons of Water, which is roughly the same Amount of Water as all of the People in the World use every 90 Days. ‡

      06-[_] We cannot Accept any such Chances. Therefore, each Row of Cisterns in such a Fortress should be Independent: so that only 210 Cisterns can be Poisoned at any one Time: beCause of being Connected with each other by Doorways at the Bases of those Cisterns. †‡

07-[_] That would still be Billions of Gallons of Polluted Water to Deal with, and no Place to put it. ‡

08-[_] I say that it is now Time to Round Up all such Poisons, and BURN them thoroughly at High Temperatures: so that they do not Pollute the Atmosphere. †§‡

09-[_] I say that we can Blame it all onto those Lying Red Jews, who are the Chief Inventors of all such Poisons: because they are the Chief Chemists in this World of Woes. †‡

10-[_] It does not matter WHOSE Fault it is for Inventing all such Abominations: because we are all to be Blamed for Allowing them to do it, which is one of the Evils that Result from having Freedom. Therefore, the one and only Reasonable Solution is to Establish **"The New RIGHTEOUS One-World Government!"**

Q-[_] The Great Question is this: **"What is the Reason for Building so many Cisterns?"**

R-[_] Well, there is no Guarantee from God nor Government that it will always go on Raining. Therefore, when it does Rain, it is Important to Capture as much Water as it as Possible, and Clean it up with Charcoal Filters, and Save in it Huge Cisterns, just in case a Great Drought should come along, and thus Ruin the whole City with its Billions of Fruit Trees, Grape Vines, Berry Bushes, Vegetable Gardens, and Flower Gardens. ‡

S-[_] So, it is Impossible to have too much Fresh Water, huh? Would all Excess Water from the Gardens drain into the Cisterns? {See: **"The LUSCIOUS All-Mineral Organic Method of Gardening!"** for the Details about how to Save the Water.}

T-[_] Well, if you, like most Americans, use an Average of 100 Gallons of Water per Day, that would be no less than a Total of 36,500 Gallons per Year, or 365,000 Gallons in 10 Years; and, if you are like most Americans, you do not even have a Garden nor Orchard to Water. Indeed, just one Fruit or Nut Tree might Drink up no less than 3,000 Gallons during one Year, if you were very Conservative with the Water by Using Swanky Mulching Rocks. A large Oak Tree might Drink 3,000 Gallons per Day, or 1,095,000 Gallons per Year. However, it normally does some Raining; but, there is no Guarantee of it. Therefore, it is Wise to be Prepared for the Worst Conditions. A Good Water Supply is a matter of National Security, and Personal Security. ‡

U-[_] I Understand the Need for a Good Water Supply; but, I do not Understand WHY we should have to Build BILLIONS of Large Cisterns, just to have International Security.

V-[_] Well, you would not want to be the Victim of a Water Shortage, just for the Lack of a little Work with some Machines, would you? It is the Ounce of Prevention that is Worth thousands of Pounds of Cures: beCause, what can be Done in this World of

(The Equitable Wage System!)

Wonders without WATER? Indeed, you would have to Boil your Eggs in Sea Water, and also Wash your Clothes in it — that is, IF you could figure out HOW to Transport Ocean Water Inland by thousands of Miles, and then Distribute it among Billions of People! †§‡

W-[_] Water is the Life of almost everything, and Fresh Clean Pure Living Water is very Rare in this World of Woes: beCause of Pollution from Acid Rains, Factories, Spilled Oils, Gases, Solvents, Detergents, House Cleansers, Dishwaters, Bleach, Chlorine, Drugs, and whatever is Dumped in the Water by Capitalists, Socialists, Communists, Fascists, and other Ists — even a whole List of tens of thousands of Capitalist Abominations that Jesus Christ Lived Happily without, O Wallabies and Kangaroos! ‡

X-[_] X-amount of Small Swanky Fortresses could be Built on smaller Outcroppings of Bedrock, all around the World. Indeed, there is no Need for HUGE Swanky Fortresses, which cover 10,000 square Miles of Land, when 16 square Miles would be Ideal, as in 4 Miles by 4 Miles, which could contain at least 40,000 People, which is a Moderately-Sized City, which would have everything that everyone Needs, which could be Built in 4 Large Terraces, each of which is 220 feet Wide. In other Words, the Hotel in the Center of the City would have 4 Terraces on the Inside, and 4 Terraces surrounding it on the Outside, making it 2,200 feet Wide on one Side of the Hotel, or a Total of 6,600 feet from the Outermost Terrace Base to the Outermost Terrace Base, plus some Space in the Center for a Golf Course: beCause X-amount of People like to Play with their little Balls. And then there should be a Flat Space around the Outside of the Hotel, beyond the 4 Terraces that surround the Outside of the Hotel, between those Terraces and the Greater Terraces of the Swanky Castle, which surrounds the Hotel, which also has its Inside and Outside Terraces, which could each be 440 feet Wide and 100 feet High: so that the Castle is up High Above the Hotel and Fortress, which Fortress surrounds the Castle in lower Terraces, similar to the Terraces at the Hotel, which are 60 feet Tall and 220 feet Wide. In other Words, there would be Open Spaces between the Swanky Hotels, Castles, and Fortresses for Livestock: beCause it is Unrealistic to Imagine that People are going to Live without Eating Flesh and Cheese and other Animal Products, now that we are Addicted to all such Stinking Things. Therefore, we might as well just Plan on having them, and Properly so, as in Swanky-Quality Smoked Turkeys and Pheasants with Biscuits and Gravy: beCause God will Give to us the Desires of our Hearts. †§‡

Y-[_] In Yesteryears, that Plan would have Worked very Well; but, now we have Factory Farms, whereby there might be 100,000 Hogs on just one Farm, which Stinks for Miles around with Capitalist Aroma, which we cannot Live without, which should be Located in the Center of that Fortress that was Described above — I Mean that it should be in the Center of the Swanky Hotel, Surrounding that Golf Course: so that there is no Escaping from the Wonderful Fragrance that Surrounds it. Indeed, even the Baby Jesus would Love it, and the Apostle Paul would Praise it: beCause the "Shambles" could be well-stocked with Bacon, Sausages, and Hickory-smoked Hams! Indeed, it is not Possible for us to have a High Standard of Living without LOTS of Pig Meat to Eat. Yes, just Ask God, if you Doubt it. †§‡§§ (See *First Corinthians 10:25, KJV.*)

Z-[_] The Zeal of **The Worldwide People's Revolution!**® will make all such Things Possible; but, that is not to say that any of those Plans would be IDEAL Ways to Live:

beCause that has yet to be Proven in a Courtroom with a Righteous Judge in Charge of it, who is Seeking the most Pure Wholesome Provable Truths, and **"The IDEAL Place to Live!"** Yes, such a Place must be Constructed: beCause it does not yet Exist. ‡

10-08 [_] Why is it that the Holy Spirit Speaks to you in Verses that are Numbered with a 7?

10-09 [_] Well, that is beCause 7 is the Perfect Number, as in 7 Days per Week, and 52 of those Weeks per Year, whereby 5 plus 2 equals 7. (See my New Calendar in: **"For the Love of Money!"**) Then there are Seven Candlesticks, 7 Spirits of God, 7 Churches, and 7 Special Archangels, among other 7's. {See: **"The Seven Basic Spiritual Building Blocks of LIFE!"**}

10-10 [_] So, O Elected King, if 7 is the Perfect Number, WHY does your New RIGHTEOUS One-World Government have 6 High Priests from 6 Major Religions, plus 60 Elected Kings from 60 Major Nations, plus a Maximum of 600 Elected Governors from Minor Nations, Provinces, and Islands of the Seas? Indeed, that seems to be Contradictory to me. ‡

10-11 [_] Well, when you Add on the Elected Righteous King to the 6 High Priests, who is a Special "Priest," himself, you might say, who is Above all of the Elected Officials, who also gives his Special Speeches, that also makes 7, whose Wisdom is Equal to that of 10 Elected Kings; and therefore, when you add on 10 to the 60 Elected Kings, that also makes 70, whose Wisdom is also Equal to that of 100 Elected Governors, which would make 700 of them, which is also a Perfect Number, as in 777. Therefore, it is Equal to 7 High Priests, 70 Elected Kings, and 700 Governors, if that has any Special Meaning to anyone. It certainly has no Special Meaning to me: beCause I am not Superstitious about Numbers, as many People are, who Believe in Lady Luck, Lucky Numbers, 7 Churches, 7 Hills in Rome, 7 Ages, and all such Nonsense, which does not Fit in with Realities at all. Indeed, Milk Cows normally have just 4 Teats, even if Elephants, Horses and Goat have only 2, each: beCause the Cows have 2 Extra Teats for People to Suck on, while the Goats have just enough Teats for Twin Kid Goats to Suck on, while a Feral Hog has about 20 Teats for her Babies, in 2 Rows, while a Bitch might have a dozen Teats for her Pups; but, all of those Animals have only 4 Legs. Therefore, 4 must be the Perfect Number. Indeed, even People have just 4 Limbs, as do Chickens, Ducks, Peacocks, Pheasants, Turkeys, and all other Birds, Frogs, and lesser Animals like Squirrels, Skunks, Rats, Cats, and Monkeys. Therefore, we could Conclude that 7 is an Odd Number, and an Unlucky Number, also, even though it does Fit into the 364-day Year with 52 Weeks with 4 Weeks in each of 13 Months, whereby 1 plus 3 equals 4 — such as the 4 Phases of the Moon, which is some more Pure Nonsense: because the Moon is constantly Changing its Reflections of Sunlight. †§‡

10-12 [_] The Complications of Money have only been made that Way by those Lying Red Jews, who could make a simple Thing — such as Fair Wages — into something so Complicated that almost no one on the Earth can Understand it. After all, if Labor must be Divided into no less than 10 Varieties, even as were Outlined in Verse 08-08-01—10, so much Confusion would arise from it as to Sink the Capitalist Ship, which is already Severely Leaking and taking on Water, which the Politicians are having a Difficult Time Bailing Out with their Dainty Teacups, when they should be using 20-gallon Buckets, and Moving 4 Times as Quickly! Indeed, the Best Solution for that Complicated Monetary System, is to Pay all Politicians Minimum Wages — such as 10$ per Hour — until those Swanky Fortresses get Built. Moreover, all of the Voluntary

(The Equitable Wage System!)

Working Soldiers could be Contented with only 20$ per Hour, if they are doing something Productive; and simply go to Bed and REST, whenever they get too Tired to Work: beCause they can Work in RELAYS, whereby one Team Works for 2 Hours, and then another Team takes over the Work, whereby the Work can get Done as Quickly as Possible: so that everyone can be Living in their **"Beautiful Swanky PALACES"** as Quickly as Possible: so that everyone can Rest in Peace, while their Luscious All-Mineral Organic Gardens are Growing, which will no longer Need any Guards: beCause they will be within the Borders of those **"GLORIOUS Swanky Hotels Castles and Fortresses!" (Beautiful Planned City States for WISE Intelligent Well-Educated People with Common Sense and Good Understanding!) By The Worldwide People's Revolution!®** Book 019. Yes, that will Greatly Simplify everything. †§‡

10-13 [_] I Propose that we Simplify it even more, by doing away with ALL Forms of Money: beCause it does not Require Money for making Beer, for Example: beCause it only Requires the Proper Tools, Ingredients, Temperatures, and Time to Brew. Therefore, if **"The New RIGHTEOUS One-World Government"** has all of the Necessary Nolij and Ingredients for Brewing that Beer, that Good Government can make it by the one-million-gallon Cistern full, according as it is Wanted, and People can Drink it by the Barrel, if they Want it, until they Conclude that it is Better by a hundred Times to Drink a little Fresh Cold Grape Juice, Orange Juice, Mango Juice, or some other Fresh Fruit Juice, which will not only Nourish the Body, as it should; but, it will also Help to Keep the Bowels Working Properly, and Satisfy a Person's Hunger for something Cold and Sweet, which is a Natural Craving for Babies and Adults. †§‡

10-14 [_] Surely we could Produce an Abundance of all Good Things, if we had **"Seven Great Armies of Working Soldiers"** at our Command! Indeed, if more 100% Pure Grape Juice is Wanted, we can Plant several Million Acres with Grapes, and do whatever is Necessary to make them Produce, with or without the Help of any Gods, who will likely be Happy to see us Drinking Fresh Grape Juices, rather than Drinking Beers, Whiskeys, Rums, Wines, and other Poisons. In Fact, we can Plant the whole Earth with Fruit Trees, Berry Bushes, Grape Vines, and Good Winter Squashes, which Produce most Abundantly, which are the Least Bothered by Bad Bugs and Birds. Yes, **"The Swanky Association of Botanists and Organic Gardeners"** can Work Together to Produce Disease-free Fruits, and a million New Varieties of them! After all, have you ever Eaten a Mint-flavored Deglet Noor Date? How about a Liquorish-flavored Peach? I like a Butterscotch Strawberries on a Mango Smoothie. †§‡

10-15 [_] Well, there is a World of Opportunities to Produce all Kinds of Wonderful Things, if People would only Sacrifice their Pride and Foolishness on the Altar of Reason and Logic. My Heroes are those People who Seek Out and Explore the World for Provable Truths, who cannot be Debunked by Capitalist Hogs, who can only be Motivated by GREED, who have little or no Empathy for other People, who were perhaps Born to be SERVANTS, who have no Interest in being Masters, who only Want to Earn an Honest Living, and Love their Naaberz as much as they Love themselves, which everyone should be doing, even if they were Born to be MASTERS, who should be the First to Confess the Goodness of United Effort, which, by itself, does Away with Money: beCause it is not Needed nor Wanted for True Prosperity, which Requires BILLIONS of those Swanky Cisterns for SECURITY, which neither Capitalism, Socialism, Communism, nor any other Isms have Built: beCause their Motives and Objectives are NOT in Favor of the Masses of People, who would much Prefer to be Living within those **"GLORIOUS Swanky Hotels Castles and Fortresses!"** However, if anyone Doubts it, just take a Poll among those People who have "red" my Inspired Books. Yes, I dare say that not one of them will Object to my Proposals, which are most Reasonable, which will get RID of Pollutions, Poverty, Politicians, Police DEPARTments, Prisons, most Professors, most Preachers, and most of the Pumpkinheads, who are known as the Capital P People. {See www.Amazon.com for: **"The PRAYERS of Pumpkinheads!" (Even God Needs a little Humor to Cheer himself Up!) By The Worldwide People's Revolution!® Book 007.**}

— Chapter 11 —

Working for the Fun of it!

11-01 [_] I can Remember when I was just a Boy, about 10 Years of Age, and my Daddy was Building a Shed for Horses on his 1,200-acre Ranch, in Montana, which had about 30 Buildings on it; and therefore, being Young and Full of Life, I found it very Rewarding to be a Part of what was Happening on the Ranch, and without any Pay: beCause there was no Pay, except for something to Eat and Drink, and some Clothes to Wear, and a Bed to Sleep in, and a Roof over my Head, and Heat from the Furnace during those very COLD Winter Days — all of which seemed to be Fair Swanky Wages to me at the Time: beCause I got to Eat all that I Wanted to, and to Drink all of the Milk that I Wanted to: because I got to Milk the Cows, and Grind the Wheat for making Whole Wheat Bread, which I also made for the Fun of it: beCause it Tasted 10 Times Better than any Bread in **"The Public School of IGNERUNT FQLZ!"** Yes, it was Extremely GOOD, when Compared with their White Devitalized bread, which was not even Worthy to be Capitalized with a Capital B — as in Satisfying Whole Wheat Bread that has been made from Organically-grown Wheat, on Land that has been Treated with the Proper Amount of Horse Manure and Cow Manure, which has Real Wholesome Natural Flavors that one cannot even Discover, nowadays: beCause, even if the Cow Manure was put on the Land, it would come from Cows that were Fed Abominations, including Chicken Litter, Growth Hormones, and God knows what else! Thus some of those Cows have Lumps, Tumors, Abscesses, Cancers, and Various Sicknesses and Diseases: beCause they are Far Removed from their Distant Relatives that used to Live on the Great Plains, who had NONE of those Diseases, whose Udders were not Dragging on the Ground, like some Dairy Cattle, nowadays. †§‡

11-02 [_] O Elected King, I can also well Remember when I was a Young Man, who Visited the Mennonites, who were Building a Big Barn, and all within just 3 Days, which I also Discovered was a LOT of Fun: beCause of the Accomplishment of TEAMWORK, which gives to a Person a Great Feeling of Satisfaction, just as long as the Wooden Barn does not Burn Down, like that Barn did within a Week, which was Heartbreaking! Yes, it was an Accident with a Kerosene Lamp, which Happened while the Father was Packing some Buckets of Milk to his House, and his Workhorse had reached over a short Wall, and knocked the Lamp onto the Floor of the Barn, which was Naturally Covered with Straw, which Ignited within a Second, and Spread throughout the Barn in less than one Minute: because a little Breeze was Blowing through it. Yes, you could Falsely Accuse some Hebrew God, or even some Greek God for that Happening; but, it was the

(The Equitable Wage System!)

Fault of that Workhorse, who was Naturally Ignorant, who did not Realize the Grave Danger of doing what he did: beCause he Killed himself and 3 other Workhorses and a dozen Cows: beCause the Farmer did not See what was Happening, until it was far too Late to Stop it. Indeed, the Barn was Located too far away from the House, whereby the Fire was not Noticed, until it was too Late. However, being Good-hearted Mennonites, their Naaberz simply came Together and Built another Barn for that Farmer, who was not even a Mennonite; but, he was a Good Naaber, who had Treated the Mennonites Well, and did Justice for them, who also had Mercy on him when he Needed it. Therefore, there were no Bad Feelings among them, nor did anyone Accuse that Poor Farmer of being STUPID, except for myself: beCause I Thought about it, and thus Concluded that he should have known that Horses are sometimes Mischievous Creatures, who can also figure out how to Escape from their Pens and Corrals: because they are quite Intelligent Creatures, and some are Geniuses, you might say, who are Smarter than their Owners! But, in that Case, it was a very Sad Story: because, neither he nor the Mennonites came to a Rational Conclusion, whereby they might have Determined to Build a SOLID STONE Barn, without any Wood in it: beCause of using Steel Gates, Doors, and Windows, whereby not even a Fire would Greatly Effect the Barn, even if all of the Straw were Burned, which could be Stored in a Separate Stone Dome, which is Attached to the Stalls with the Horses, which can have Stone Walls between them, which are not so Tall that the Horses cannot See Over them: beCause Horses like to Talk with each other. Indeed, they do not Appreciate being made into Prisoners, nor into Slaves: beCause they are Communal Creatures, much like Men with Harems in Saudi Arabia, which is Acceptable to them: beCause it is another SIN of Wealth and Prestige, which would not be the Case without that Filthy Stinking Money. †§‡

11-03 [_] Well, I certainly Agree that all such Wooden Barns are Potential Disasters. Therefore, did you Volunteer to Help them to Rebuild the Barn that Burned?

11-04 [_] No. But, I did Try to Explain to them what was Needed for True Prosperity. However, they did not Understand Stonework, nor did they Believe that God Created all of those Billions of Trees to NOT be Used Wisely for Building Houses and Barns, even as most Americans Believe: beCause they have never Seen Proper Houses nor Proper Barns, much less any of those **"GLORIOUS Swanky Hotels Castles and Fortresses!"**

11-05 [_] So, the Happiness that came to you by United Effort, by Working with those Mennonites, was Shattered, you might say; and their Unbelief in the Inspired Words of Jesus Christ must have been Extremely Depressing: beCause they Profess to Believe in him. (See *Matthew 7:22—29.*)

11-06 [_] Yes, it was very Depressing, and so much so that I had to Move Away from them. After all, the Art of Stonework is more Honorable than Building Wooden Firetrap Buildings. However, if that Stonework is not done Properly, a Person can easily Construct another Potential Natural Disaster for an EARTHQUAKE, whereby the Rocks can Fall on your own Head! Yes, there was just such an Example in Italy, where Ancient Buildings came Crumbling Down: beCause those Poor People did not Understand what was Required for SECURE Houses, which are called: **"Swanky Stone Dome Home Complexes!"** Yes, as far as I know, there is not even ONE such House in the whole World! And the Reason for it is quite Obvious — almost no one could AFFORD to Buy nor Build such a House: beCause the Solid Stone Walls must be at least 10 feet THICK, just to make them Earthquake Resistant, Self-air-conditioned, Sound-proof,

Bomb-proof, and Insurance-proof. Indeed, with such Horrible Bombs as we have, such Roofs should be no less than 20 feet THICK, and in several different Layers of Rocks, Sand, Gravel, Clay, and more Rocks, and especially Granite Rocks, which are the Hardest ones, which are more Resistant to those Hateful Bombs, which can also be Installed in the Concrete and Rock Domes, which should have Extra Secure Bedroom Domes, whereby People can Sleep in Peace, even if the Bombs do fall on them, which would have little or no Great Effects on all such Domes, even though they would mess up the Topsoil and Trees in the Gardens, which a Wicked Anti-Christ False Cover-up Government would no doubt Bomb with NAPALM, whereby they would Attempt to Destroy all of the Trees, if nothing else: because they are Spiritual COWARDS, who would not Show their Faces at: **"The Great Worldwide TELEVISED Court HEARING"**: beCause of Knowing for a Fact that they are Unjust, Wicked, Greedy SELFISH LYING RED JEWS, who should be EXTERMINATED! †§‡

11-07 [_] Maybe they have their Mean Natures beCAUSE of being Mistreated so Meanly during the Jewish HoloHOAX, whose Chief Persecutors were some more Lying Zionist Red Jews! Yes, it was Jews against Jews, which can be Proven in a Courtroom. Zionist Jews were in Charge of it, even as they are Presently in Charge in the Land of Israel, who Mistreat the Palestinians, who Naturally have their Excuses: because they are Good at Inventing Excuses, even as they have Invented Excuses for not Attending **"The Great Worldwide TELEVISED Court HEARING!"** Yes, just Watch and See for yourself that I am RIIT! †§‡

11-08 [_] O Elected King, you are no doubt Right about that: beCause those Lying Red Jews could now bring YOU to Court, and Prove your Books to be WRong, if they are wRong; but, I would say that they are RIIT, and that no Lying Red Jew can Prove them to be Rong. However, even if he or she can, we will only have to Modify the Books, in order to make them Correct, which will be an easy Editing Job. After all, that is WHY we have Computers for making Corrections, even as you have had to Change your Pen Names, just to Conform to the Wishes of Amzon.com and whomever might have been Offended with Master Mark Revolutionary Twain, Junior, whom they Assumed was Mark Twain, himself, who is YOU, Reincarnated; and Adolf Dictator Hitler, Junior; and The Reverend Doctor Billy Graham, Junior; and Sir Winston William Shakingspears, Junior, whom you have Impersonated for the Glory of Literary Arts. †§‡

11-09 [_] Well, whomever I am, it is more likely that God is Correct, that I am the Man with the Spirit of Elijah, who has come to set the Household of Israel in Order, and get them Prepared for the Second Coming of Jesus Christ, which will Naturally be Extremely Difficult for Unbelieves to Accept, in spite of the Provable Facts being on my Side! Yes, all of the Arguments concerning all Important Subjects seem to be on my Side of every Issue, just as they should be. After all, I am on the Side of Truths, and therefore **"The Swanky Sword of Divine Truths"** is on my Side, and nobody can Withstand it. Moreover, if they Attempt to Resist it, they will only be Cutting Off their own Tale of Lies: beCause no one can Fight Against the Sword of Truths, and Win! However, if you are one of those Silly People, who Vainly Imagines that you can Fight Against it, and Win, why not DEMAND **"The Great Worldwide TELEVISED Court HEARING,"** along with the other Brave Souls, if you are not all Spiritual COWARDS? ‡

11-10 [_] O Elected King, when Children are Young and Full of Ambitions, they are Happy to Work for nothing; but, when they Grow Up and get Married, they come to Realize that they must Obtain a LOT of Money, unless they Want to Live in someone's Attic or Basement Apartment;

(The Equitable Wage System!)

or, worse yet, in the Backseat of some Used Car, without so much as a Bathroom, which would only have to be a little Room with a Shower Bucket and a Dung Bucket, which might Cost all of 30$, if such a Person cannot Discover a Used Plastic Pickle Bucket in some Dumpster behind the Burger King Restaurant, for FREE; and then it might Cost 5$ for a Cheap Value, one or 2 Flanges, depending on how Strong the Capitalist Bucket is, a 2-inch Pipe to Fit the bottom Flange and the Value, called a Nipple; plus some Rubber for Seals, which can be made of a used Inner Tube for a Tire, plus 4 Bolts, Washers, and Nuts at a Hardware Store. You could Borrow the Tools at some Welding Shop to put it all together, and even Beg the Welder to make a Hole in the Bottom of the Bucket for the Water to run through. Otherwise, you might Trade some Work for it, such as Sweeping up the Floor, or Cleaning his Dirty "Restroom." †

11-11 [_] Well, just Think about how HAPPY those Young People would be, if they had a Fatherly Good Government, which Supplied them with all of the Necessary Building Materials for Building those **"GLORIOUS Swanky Hotels Castles and Fortresses!"** Yes, they would naturally need Architects, Engineers, Designers, Construction Workers, and Professional People to Assist them to get it Done Correctly, who are now Unemployed — Thanks to the Evil Empire, which has only ONE Way to Raise anyone's Standard of Living, and that is by Producing and Selling more TRASH. Yes, if you are Poor and Unemployed, you must either Invent some Thing to SELL, or else you must Work for someone who is Producing such Things for Sale, or else you must make a Slave of yourself to some other Capitalist, who might be Servicing such BAD Capitalist Products — such as a Greasy Mechanic's Job, which might seem to be Glamorous, until you get Hurt, or even Killed by it! Indeed, at the very least, you will never have Clean Hands, again, unless you QUIT; but, why would you Want to Quit such a "Good Job," which might Pay twice as much as Washing Dishes in some Greasy Restaurant? Otherwise, you could go to Work at a Sawmill, Lumberyard, Rock Quarry, Cement Factory, Welding Job, Butchering Hogs, or Gathering Chickens in one of those very Hot DUSTY Chicken Houses, where you must Bend Over Catching 5 Chickens for each Hand, in order to Stuff those Chickens into Cages, until you have Gathered up no less than 10,000 of them during one Night, while Working with other Miserable Mexicans, who are also Gathering up their 10,000 Chickens, each: beCause, if you do not get a Sufficient Number of them Gathered up, your Pay will be Docked! Meanwhile, a Lawyer can Charge you a thousand Times as much Money for her "Services," who has no Idea what it is like to Gather Up Chickens in such a Hell Hole. Therefore, with just one Night of that Capitalist Mistreatment, you will be Ready to Consider Joining the Army, while Hoping that you never Actually get into Combat with some Enemy Army, who found themselves in the same Predicament, being Poor, Unemployed, and Desperate for some MONEY — all beCause you do not have your own Beautiful Swanky Palace to Live in, where there is Eternal Employment in those Luscious Gardens, Vineyards, Orchards, Home-craft Workshops, Sales Shops, and wherever. In Fact, it might Require 400 Years to get all of those Swanky Castles Built, if they are very Artistic about it, which they could be. However, even without Swanky Castles, there will still be "Eternal" Employment, even without any Money: beCause there is Fine Hand-crafted Furniture to be made for all of the Houses, which can take a Long Time, if it is done Correctly, and thus be more Valuable. ‡

11-12 [_] O Elected King, whomever would not Vote for you to be their Elected King must have a 2x4 Board up their Rectum, as in WRECKED-HIS-BRAINS, even though it could be said better. But, I cannot Think of just HOW to say it like Shakingspears might say it. †§

11-13 [_] Well, it is sufficient to say that my Opposition will Wreck themselves in a Head-on Collision with Reality when the Rain STOPS, and there is nothing to EAT, which could have a Great Effect on their Thinking Apparatuses, and might even get them Converted to the Provable Truths that I have been Promoting for more than 30 Years! After all, Elijah had a Good Plan for Correcting those Israelites. (See *First Kings 17,* in whatever Version you like. It is quite a Story.)

11-14 [_] O Elected King, let us Hope to God that it does not have to Happen, once again: beCause one Time of such a Great Famine should be Sufficient to Teach that Lesson to Humanity.

11-15 [_] Well, as always, the People have a CHOICE: beCause no such Great Famine must Come; but, if almost all of the People do not Repent, something Drastic will have to Happen, and I may not Live through it, myself. After all, there is no Guarantee for what a Day might bring forth; but, for Sure, People will Reap whatever they Sow, which may be 200 Atomic Bombs on their Heads! Nevertheless, I do HOPE that it does not come to that; but, I would not be Surprised if it did: beCause some Americans are some of the most STUPID People who ever Lived! ‡ {See www.Amazon.com for: **"Are Americans the Most STUPID People who ever Lived?" (HOW Working People can PROSPER and Live in PEACE Under the Rulership of a RIGHTEOUS KING!) By The Worldwide People's Revolution!® Book 047.**}

— Chapter 12 —

The Price that People Pay for Rejecting Truths

12-01 [_] O Elected King, this will be a very Sad Book to Read, during the Future, if the Big Bombs should Drop on **"The Divided States of United Lies!" (The so-called "United States of North America" in Disguise!) By The Worldwide People's Revolution!®** Book 058. Therefore, would it not be Better to Edit OUT all such Spooky Prophecies?

12-02 [_] Well, if only it would Spook them into Doing what is RIIT for themselves and others, it would be Good. However, I Agree with you — that it would be a very Sad Book to Read, during the Future, if the Big Bombs Drop on us: beCause, the very Evil Thing that we have Feared the Most will have Come on us, which would be another one of those Immortalized Days that the People of the World could never Forget — at least we would HOPE that they would never Forget it. However, Elijah probably Thought the very same Thing about that Great Famine, and Hoped to God that it would not have to Happen again. But, it Appears that it will have to Happen once again — except that this Time it is much Different: beCause of those Hideous Weapons of Mass Destruction, which are now in the Hands of some very Untrustworthy People — such as Vladimir Putin and the Leaders of **"The Divided States of United Lies,"** who are Trigger-happy, as the saying goes, who Fire First, and Ask Questions Later, which is a BAD Way to Conduct themselves, when it not only Possible; but, much more Practical, for them to DEMAND: **"The Great Worldwide TELEVISED Court HEARING,"** which might seem like

(The Equitable Wage System!)

a Painful Thing to those Lying Zionist Red Jews and the Red Jew Sympathizers; but, as Painful as it might be, it will not be nearly as Painful as Suffering through a Great Atomic NIGHTMARE! YES, THAT IS THE PUNISHMENT, which God Ordains for the Rejecters of Truths without any Justifiable Causes! Therefore, BE WARNED, and FLEE from those most Vulnerable Places that are like Sodom and Gomorra!

12-03 [_] And just Exactly WHAT were the Sins of Sodom and Gomorra, which Doomed them?

12-04 [_] Well, their Chief Sin was a DIETARY Sin, called "Gluttony," whereby they were STUFFED with Foods, which put PRESSURE in their Lower Bowels: beCause of Eating Constipating Foods, whereby the Men Appeared to be Pregnant, even though they were NOT; but, they were Stuffed with Foods, being very much like many Americans, who have been Deceived by Satan, the Devil, who also Deceived Mother Eve in the Garden of Eden, and got her to Eat the Forbidden Food, which Symbolized all Future Forbidden Foods, which are many. ‡ {See www.Amazon.com for: **"Did God or Satan Ordain Medical Doctors??" (Ask Huck Finn and/or Nigger Jim: because neither Tom Sawyer nor Judge Thatcher would Know!) By The Worldwide People's Revolution!® Book 022.**}

12-05 [_] O Elected King, what were some of the other Sins of Sodom and Go-more-of-it?

12-06 [_] Well, the Rich ones were all PUFFED UP with Great PRIDE for their Riches, rather than being Humble and Thankful to God for whatever they had: beCause they could have just as easily been Born in the Heart of Africa, in some Hot Sweaty Jungle with Various Snakes to Torment them. Otherwise, they could have been Born in Alaska, or Greenland, whereby they might have been Deprived of some of their Riches. However, as it was, the Plains around Sodom and Gomorra were very Fertile and Productive, whereby they had more than enough to EAT; and therefore, they got themselves into the Cooking Pit with all Kinds of Spices that they might have Discover, which they also Bought from Travelers and Sailors, who Transported Goods from India by Way of the Indian Ocean and the Red Sea, which were Moved to Sodom and Gomorra by Camels: because it was not that far from the Red Sea. Moreover, they Mistreated the Poor People in Sodom and Gomorra, which Inspired God to say: *"Behold, this was the Iniquity of your Sister Sodom, even Pride, Fullness of Foods, and an Abundance of Idleness was in her and in her Daughters, who Hated Gardening; neither did she Strengthen the Hands of the Poor and Needy People, who had no Land to Exploit, who were made into the Slaves of the Rich People, which Thing I Hate, says the Supreme Ruler your God. Yes, they were Haughty, and Committed Abominations in front of me, whereby the Men were having Anal Penetrations, which are Filthy, Nasty, Stinking, Disease-spreading Acts of the Sons of Belial, which I Hate: because there are Better Ways for them to Relieve themselves, which the Greeks have Discovered, who are Wiser People, who have no such Sodomites among them. Therefore, I took those Sodomites away as I saw Necessary to Warn the People of the World during Future Generations, who might Learn about them: because, during the Last Days, before the Second Coming of the Anointed One, the Perverse Men will be doing similar Evil Things, when they could be having Frot Sex, like the Greeks, and thus Avoid Damnation: beCause of Practicing Fidelity, which I Love above all Things, and so should you: beCause it will Prevent all such Whoredoms."* — The NMV of Ezekiel 16:49—50. (See www.Man2ManAlliance.org for the Details.)

12-07 [_] So, O Elected King, are you Confident that God is not Offended by Frot Sex?

12-08 [_] Well, are YOU Offended by it? Can you Rightfully Deny that it would be a VAST Improvement over Sodomy, Adultery, Drug Addictions, Gluttony, Drunkenness, and Evil Things that arise from a Lack of Love and Affection? Indeed, X-amount of Men were Born GAY, even as X-amount of Animals, including about 80% of all African Elephants, which we have a Good Example for HOW to Deal with it, except that they might not Practice Fidelity. Indeed, a more Thorough, Scientific Study would have to be made of them, whereby we might Learn the Truth about it. ‡

12-09 [_] So, are you Seeking to Justify American Sodomites by Studies of Elephants, O King?

12-10 [_] No, I have no Justifications at all for any Sodomites, who need to Learn about FROT Sex, whereby they might Avoid all such Evil Nasty Acts, which are not Necessary for having the Best Sex in the World, according to those People who Practice it. Go talk with them, if you Doubt it. (See the Link in Verse 12-06.)

12-11 [_] So, O Elected King, what would the Doctor Reverend Billy Graham have to say about all such Sensual Acts of Fidelity?

12-12 [_] Well, he was Obviously Contented with the Way that he was Born, which was Good: beCause he also Believed in Fidelity, as far as I know. Moreover, I am not Interested in any Slanderous Rumors to the Contrary: beCause his Team always went Together, around the World, and Protected each other from any Infidelities. Therefore, Billy Graham was not the Ordinary Run-of-the-Mill Evangelist, like so-and-so, who Preached against Homosexuals for 20+ Years, and got Caught in Bed with one of them, somewhere in Europe. He should have been Honest with himself and other People, and Confessed that X-amount of Men are Born GAY, which is no Sin; but, to Practice Sodomy, which is Anal Penetrations with Penises, is a Major Sin, right next to Adultery, Murder, and Rape — all of which can be Avoided by Greek Frot Sex, without Sinning, and thus without any Condemnation from God nor from Honest People, who Understand the Overwhelming POWER of Testosterone in a Horny Young Man, who should Learn HOW to Relieve himself without Sinning, which includes the Act of Masturbation, which is much Better than Raping someone. ‡

12-13 [_] Well, O King, if you say so, I will have to Agree. After all, a Person might spend a lot of Time in some Hateful Prison for Committing Rape, just for Failing to use his Hand to Relieve himself, even as any Monkey or Ape would do, or even as a Horse or Bull would do, by Rubbing himself on the Ground. However, I Fail to Understand what Connection there is between FAIR Swanky WAGES and Frot Sex! Can you Explain that to us? ‡

12-14 [_] Well, I cannot see any Direct Connection; but, there might be a Connection, since it would be Extremely Difficult for any Gay Young Man to Discover another Gay Young Man who might Practice FIDELITY: beCause most People have not Filled Out nor Filed **"The Complete SURVEYS of our VALUES!" (SURVEYS of Religious Spiritual Political Governmental Sexual Social Moral Economic Business Labor Habitual and Miscellaneous VALUES!) By The Worldwide People's Revolution!®** Book 059.

12-15 [_] O Elected King, I would Think that you would be Ashamed to even Address any such Subjects as Sodomy, in spite of the Fact that more than a MILLION Young American Men

(The Equitable Wage System!)

Contract AIDS, each Year: beCause of NOT Practicing Frot Sex, which seems to be a Great Shame on the News Broadcasters, Teachers, Preachers, Priests, Professors, Politicians, and other Professionals, who should be Referring those Young Men to your Inspired Books, which are very Frank and Honest about a LOT of Important Subjects, which is Exactly HOW we will Expect you to be when you are Seated on your Royal Golden Throne in: **"The Great World TEMPLE of PEACE,"** in Jerusalem, where all Important Subjects will be Addressed by Honest People, rather than Pay the High Price for Rejecting Truths without any Justifiable Causes.

— Chapter 13 —

There will be Peace in the Valley!

13-01 [_] So, O Elected King, do you Believe that Menkind will Eventually Learn what is GOOD for us, and thus Obtain Peace with GOD, who is ALL that is GOOD? Moreover, WHY did God not Explain a few Things about the Nature of Men to Moses, whereby many of those Sins could have been Avoided? Did God Actually WANT us to Experience all of these EVILS in this World of Woes, just to Teach certain Good Lessons to us?

13-02 [_] Well, the Quickest Way for us to Establish True Peace on the Earth, is to do Away with all Money and the Great Pride that comes from having False Riches — such as those Stinking Noisy Polluting Vehicles, which give to Ignorant People a False Sense of Pride and Power that they should not have, just by Stepping on their Gas Pedals, and Zooming along on the Highways, and Especially if they have some very HOT "Hotrod," which might be the Latest Abomination in the Nostrils of God, who could have Inspired Jesus to Talk about it, or to Prophesy about it; but, it would likely have been Misunderstood. After all, it was the Will of God that our Spirits should be Tested by Satan, the Devil, who has Certainly Discovered those People who Love his Lies — one of which is the "Goodness" of Cars, Vans, Pickups, Trucks, Buses, Motorboats, Motorcycles, Motor Scooters, Snowmobiles, Snow Blowers, Chainsaws, Weed-eaters, Garden Tillers, 4-Wheelers, and Especially AIRPLANES, which make it Possible for us to Fly across the Oceans and Lands in Hours, rather than in Days, Weeks, or even Months, as it used to be when the Sailors used SAILS in the Wind. Now we have Hydrogen to use, which is Clean and Permissible in Ships and Airplanes, except that I know of none that Use it. Perhaps it lacks Power for Airplanes? I would not know; but, I do Know that: *"Wherever there is a Will, there is a Way"* to get it Done Correctly. After all, it is Possible to HEAT UP SALT, which can Hold Heat 7 Times longer than Water: beCause the Salt can be made very HOT, while the Water only gets up to the Boiling Point. Therefore, Hot Salt could be made by Solar Power, and Stored in large Salt Blocks in Insulated Boxes in Ships of Various Sizes, which would be Harmless for the Environment, which would Generate ElecTrickery, which may be Equally as Dangerous for Human Health as other Abominations. At least Thomas Edison thought so. †‡

13-03 [_] So, O Elected King, are you Suggesting that God HATES these UGLY Rat-infested Cities of Confusion: beCause they are also Designed by Satan, the Devil?

13-04 [_] Well, just take a Good Look at any one of them from a Distance, and you will See just how UGLY they are, having Stacks of Ugly Boxes with Windows on Skyscraper, which are about as Aesthetic as PUKE! After all, it is the Results of an Evil Thing, called CAPITALISM, whereby each Person is Free to Invent such Abominations, which are known as "Eye Sores" in Europe, where they have Forbidden such Ugly Things. Indeed, can you Imagine the Italians allowing some Rich Capitalist to Build Skyscrapers all around Saint Peter's Basilica, in Rome; or all around the Florence Cathedral? NEVER! However, similar things Happened in New Yuck City, right around their Prize Cathedrals, which are Buried in the Canyons of New York City. ‡ (See *Wikipedia* for Panoramic Views of Rome and Florence, which have no Ugly Skyscrapers.)

13-05 [_] So, O Elected King, do you Believe that it is Possible for most People in the World to Agree to Build those **"GLORIOUS Swanky Hotels Castles and Fortresses,"** if it is Physically Possible to do so? Will they be Contented to be Moderately Rich? Or, will they Demand the Wealth of Bill Computer Software Gates and other Rich People?

13-06 [_] Well, the Capitalist Red Jews have forever Dangled the Cob of Corn on a String in front of the Chickens from the Roof of the Hen House with the Fishing Pole, as Mark Twain explained in one of his books, whereby the Chickens keep Chasing after it: beCause, now and then, the Rich Jews give to those Chickens a Peck on the Cob of Golden Corn. Therefore, they keep Chasing after it, and thereby Build Up the Muscles in their "Drumsticks." And that is about all that is Gained by it: beCause it is just another Red Jew Capitalist Deception, whereby the Masses of People Vainly Imagine that they too might get RICH, if they just keep Chasing after the Grand Prize; or, that they might Win the Wall Street Lottery Game, if they make the Correct Investments. However, when the Masses of People Wake Up and come to their Right Senses, they will STOP BUYING that Capitalist TRASH, and the Great False Economy will CRASH! Therefore, those Wall Street Gamblers will all go BROKE — that is, all Except those Red Jew Bankers, who will still be left with their thousands of Tons of Silver and Gold, plus the Assets of their Countless Properties, which they have Repossessed from their Debtors, who could not Pay Off their Mortgages, Credit Cards, and other Debts. Therefore, those Red Jew Bankers have themselves Covered, you might say. However, they were not Expecting any such Thing as **"The Great Worldwide TELEVISED Court HEARING,"** whereby their Sins are Exposed in the Light of Truths, whereby **"The Great False Economy is now DEBUNKED!"** Indeed, you can Help to Debunk it more Proficiently by simply not Buying any more of their Capitalist Trash. After all, the Garage and Attic and Basement are likely already Stuffed with such Junk, if not Storage Rooms in other Buildings around Town. One Person has 4 such Storage Boxes: because of not Wanting to get Rid of any of his "Precious Possessions."

13-07 [_] O Elected King, if we were Blest with the True Riches of Good Health, we would not have any Desire to Obtain nor Maintain any of those Capitalist Toys, which would be Bad News for those Rich People, who have been Depending on their Ignorant Addicted Slaves for many Years. Yes, their Chief Business is Selling Expensive DRUGS, which do not leave any Visible Trash laying around to Remind the Slaves of just how much Money that they have Wasted on all such Drugs, which do have that one Great Advantage. However, while those Slaves are Wasting their Hard-earned Money on all such Drugs, they are Depriving themselves of the True Riches, which would begin with Fresh Clean Air, Pure Living Water, Wholesome Natural Foods, Secure Houses, Crime-free Tax-free Cities, and all of the Wonderful Things that you have Proposed. I Suggest that all such People should KEEP all Used Pill Bottles in Boxes, with the Prices on

(The Equitable Wage System!)

Stickers that are Stuck to the Caps, just to Remind them of how much Money that they have Wasted on those MediSINZ, which you have not Wasted, your Honor: beCause of never Buying even ONE Pill in more than 70 Years! Moreover, Billions of Wild Animals also Lived and Died without Buying any such MediSINZ: beCause they were FREE with a Capital F. ‡

13-08 [_] Well, my Friend, we only have to Follow the Money Trail, in order to Discover the True Criminals, who are those Lying Red Jews, who have Collected most of the Money in this World of Woes, while the Masses of People have only Inherited Trashy Houses, Rusty Cars, and Garages full of TRASH, after Buying their almost Worthless Houses at least 5 Times.

    A-[_] They first Borrow Money from the Bankers for Buying the Houses, which Money must be Repaid.

    B-[_] And then they Pay for those Houses 2 or 3 Times more by Paying Interest / Usury on those Loans.

    C-[_] They Pay for those Houses again by Buying Insurance.

    D-[_] They Pay for those Houses again by Paying Property Taxes.

    E-[_] They Pay for them again by Repair Bills.

    F-[_] They Pay for them again by Heating and Cooling Bills.

    G-[_] They often take out Mortgages on all such Houses, in order to put the Children through Colleges, whereby they Pay for those Houses again, even though one could Argue that it is not a House Payment; but, the House is used for "Collateral," which can be Lost to the Friendly Banker, if the Interest is not Paid.

    H-[_] Therefore, the Tax Slave, Interest Slave, Insurance Slave, Drug Slave, and Work Slave must Obtain CREDIT by getting Credit Cards, whereby he or she can Borrow more Money, just in case of an Emergency, just to make Sure that the Bankster can be Paid: because one such Slave would not Want to Lose the House for the Lack of a Payment. Therefore, it is Necessary to have CREDIT with Credit Companies, which is another Red Jew Capitalist SCAM.

    I-[_] I have Avoided all such Scams: because of not having any Credit Cards, Mortgages, Loans, nor any Dealings with Bankers, who are Legal Highway Robbers!

    J-[_] Justice Demands that all such Robbers are put Out of Business by Establishing **"The New RIGHTEOUS One-World Government!"**

    K-[_] King Jesus will do that when he Returns and Establishes his own Righteous One-World Government.

    L-[_] Lots of Laughs! "King Jesus" is an Invention of Lying Red Jews, just to get us to Believe in such Myths as he allegedly Taught, whereby we would have False Hopes, whereby we would be Deceived by such Hopes, rather than take Action to take those Lying Red Jews to COURT for their High Crimes in Low Places. †§‡

M-[_] Gaining more Money has been the Main Motive for those Lying Red Jews for thousands of Years, whose Coffers are now FULL. Meanwhile, the Masses of People are Suffering in their States of Extreme Poverty, whereby they do not even have Fresh Clean Air to Breathe, Pure Living Water to Drink, Wholesome Natural Foods to Eat, nor Secure Houses to Live in, which would have to be Fireproof, Hail-proof, Termite-proof, Rot-proof, Rat-proof, Paint-proof, Tornado-proof, Hurricane-proof, Flood-proof, Earthquake-proof, Insurance-proof, and Self-air-conditioned — all of which is Possible and most Practical.

N-[_] NONSENSE! A GOOD House can easily Burn Up, Blow Away, get Eaten by Termites, get Ruined by a Flood of Water, get Buried under a Mudslide, or just Rot Down: beCause that is the Will of God, who is in the Recycling Business. †§‡§§

O-[_] Are there no OPTIONS? Is there no Middle Ground? Could we not just Build Stronger Wooden Houses? How about Plastic Houses, which are made stronger than Steel? Could we not Save ourselves by SCIENCE, by Inventing some Capitalist Scam? Surely we could figure out how to make a smaller house for 4 times the Price, which would endure about as long as those Capitalist Cars! †§‡§§

P-[_] Most People are too Stupid to even Think about it; but, I Challenge them to Think about the many Good Reasons and Great Advantages for Building **"Beautiful Swanky PALACES"** for everyone in the World.

Q-[_] The Great Question is this: **"Will we get Paid with FAIR Swanky Wages for doing all such Work; or, will we be Robbed by Lying Red Jews, once again?"**

R-[_] **"The New RIGHTEOUS One-World Government"** will Guarantee **"The Swanky Associations of Working Soldiers"** FAIR Swanky Wages for any Work that they do: beCause, if they Do as they are Asked to Do, they will Inherit those **"Beautiful Swanky PALACES,"** which will be FAIR Swanky Wages, which no one in a RIIT Miind can Rightly Deny, which is MORE than FAIR. ‡

S-[_] Saint Peter would Confess that such Great Rewards for so little Services would be more than Fair, which might even Spoil the Children and Great Grandchildren, who would Inherit Palaces that they did not Earn, whereby they might all become Spoiled Sinners! ‡

T-[_] The Idea should be TESTED, first, before we Ruin the whole World! ‡

U-[_] I Understand that any Rebel Children can be BANISHED from all such **"GLORIOUS Swanky Hotels Castles and Fortresses,"** whereby they will not be a Problem.

(The Equitable Wage System!)

V-[_] I am a Victim of Capitalism; and therefore, I cannot See any Vision of what is Required for Escaping from the Deep Dark Pit that I have Fallen Headlong into. Therefore, the Best Solution for me is to Commit Suicide, rather than DEMAND: **"The Great Worldwide TELEVISED Court HEARING,"** whereby we might Learn what the Best Solutions for our Massive Problems ARE! ‡

W-[_] I would rather go to WAR, before Submitting to **"The Swanky Sword of Divine Truths!"** Indeed, it is simply too Em-bare-assing for me to Confess that I might have been Deceived by Satan and Sons, Incorporated! After all, I am "educated," but, not with a Capital E, or else I would have Learned all about those Wooden / Plastic Firetrap Mouse-infested Cockroach Dens, and thus would have Built a Multimillion-dollar Swanky Stone Dome Home Complex for myself, even if I needed to Borrow the Money from those Lying Zionist Red Jew Bankers: because such a House would have already Paid for itself by the Money that I would have Saved on Heating and Cooling Bills, plus Fire Insurance, plus Property Taxes, plus Painting, plus Replacing Carpets, and other Repairs, which Property Taxes would Amount to no less than 200,000$ per Year: beCause of those Marble-faced Walls, Granite-faced Floors, Stone Walls around the one-acre All-Mineral Organic Garden, and the Home-craft Workshop and Sales Shop, which the Tax Assessor would Judge to be Worth at least 2 Million Dollars! †§‡§§

X-[_] X-amount of Ignorant People will just Naturally Agree with you — that it would be Better to go to WAR, rather than Submit to **"The Swanky Sword of Divine Truths!"** However, in this Case, that War is almost Guaranteed to become an Atomic NIGHTMARE: beCause the Europeans, Russians and Chinese Peoples just Happen to Agree with our Elected King, while the British and Israelis and the Anti-Christ False Cover-up Federal Government of **"The Divided States of United Lies"** just Happen to Disagree with him, whereby they are likely to be BOMBED OFF of the Earth! Yes, it would be their Just Reward, which would Cause those Muslims to REJOICE! After all, they are Aware of the Great Satan and her Pets. †§‡

Y-[_] I am Yearning for the Great Day of REST, when Satan will be Chained Up and Cast into the Bottomless Pit, along with those Lying Zionist Red Jews, who have Orchestrated this Capitalist Empire, who set it all up in their Favor, who have made Tax Slaves, Interest Slaves, Insurance Slaves, Drug Slaves, Sex Slaves, Childcare Slaves, and Work Slaves of the Masses of People, who have no Idea HOW to Shake Off those Shackles and Chains, which Bind them Tightly in the Prison of Lies! ‡

Z-[_] The Zeal of **The Worldwide People's Revolution!®** will make it Possible to be Set FREE with a Capital F. Therefore, have Faith in All that is Good. Yes, Cling to the Strong Rope of HOPE, and do not let go: beCause it is just a Matter of Time, and **"The Swanky Sword of Divine Truths"** will Win this Spiritual Battle, and **"The New RIGHTEOUS One-World Government"** will be Established, and the World will be Living in PEACE.

13-09 [_] O Elected King, I would have never Thought that it might Happen during my Lifetime; but, now I See that it is Possible to Establish **"The New RIGHTEOUS One-World Government!" (HOW to Establish a Righteous One-World Government without Going to**

WAR!) By The Worldwide People's Revolution!® Book 056. Yes, I now See the Vision of it, which can only be Possible by Building those **"GLORIOUS Swanky Hotels Castles and Fortresses!" (Beautiful Planned City States for WISE Intelligent Well-Educated People with Common Sense and Good Understanding!) By The Worldwide People's Revolution!®,** Book 019, which will Prove to be the most Fascinating Construction Project on the Earth in all of History, whereby some of those Ugly Mountains of Rocks will be Transformed into **"Beautiful Swanky PALACES!" (A New Concept in Living Habits!) By The Worldwide People's Revolution!®** Book 066.

13-10 [_] Well, my Friend, it is the ONE and ONLY Way for us to Obtain Peace in the Valley, whereby almost everyone is Contented to be Moderately RICH, without Telling any Lies, nor Selling any Trash: beCause the Basic Necessities of Life do not Require any such Trash; but, those Necessities do Require Fresh Clean Air, Pure Living Water, Wholesome Natural Foods, Secure Stone Dome Home Complexes with Large Cisterns for Water Storage, Luscious All-Mineral Organic Gardens, Home-craft Workshops, Well-made Swanky-Quality Tools, Sales Shops, and all of the Wonderful Things that I have Proposed for each Beautiful Planned City State, which can Decide for itself what it Needs and Wants, other than those Good Things. For Example, if they are Willing to Work for it, they should have Indoors Swimming Pools, Gymnasiums, Tennis Courts, Skating Rinks, Bowling Alleys, Theaters, Concert Halls, Cathedrals, Mosques, Synagogues, Temples, Auditoriums, Museums, Royal Swanky Buffets, and whatever they Want — just as long as they do not Want any of those Noisy Stinking Polluting Abominations that fill up Junkyards and Trash Dumps: beCause those Evil Things are NOT Needed, and should not be Wanted. ‡

13-11 [_] So, O Elected King, with your Plan, the American Bisons could Roam on the Great Plains, once again, and the Tall Grasses could Grow, once again, and the Beavers could Build their Dams, once again, and the Natural Paradise of the Great Plains would Flourish, once again, whereby the Great Creator God would be Pleased with us, and thus Bless us with more Beautiful Songs, Inspiring Books, and Uplifting Sermons! Indeed, we would never again have to Hear any of those Repugnant Political Speeches: beCause all Politicians would be Retired, along with Greedy Bankers, Corrupt Lawyers, Selfish Medical Doctors, Lying Preachers, Deceptive Snakes, Stinking Painted Skunks, Vicious Bears, Ravenous Wolves, Roaring Lions, Thieving Raccoons, Sneaky Opossums, and all such Hateful Creatures. For Example, just 2 Raccoons can Ruin a Corn Patch during just one Night, by Breaking Off each Cob of Corn, just to Taste of it, rather than Eat it, and be Contented with it: beCause of not being Able to Distinguish the Difference between a Mature and Immature Cob of Corn. Therefore, they can Ruin a thousand-dollars-worth of Sweet Corn without Realizing it — NOT beCause of being EVIL Creatures, like Snakes; but, beCause of being IGNORANT Creatures, who should Live OUTSIDE of Swanky Fortresses, beyond all of the Cornfields, in the Woods, where they can be Hunted and Eaten by the Wolves, which is what they are Good for. Therefore, the Good Creatures can be Gathered into the Fortresses, and the Evil Creatures can be Cast Out of it; and thus we can Live in Peace. ‡

13-12 [_] Well, whatever is Best for us can be Proven at: **"The Great Worldwide TELEVISED Court HEARING!" (That Great Meeting of the Most Intelligent Minds!) By The Worldwide People's Revolution!®** Book 041. Yes, if you have a Better Solution, please Present it to us by Means of the *Chain of Command,* which I have Revealed in: **"The Washington Journal is a FARCE!"** Book 006.

(The Equitable Wage System!)

13-13 [_] O Elected King, I have a Solution for those TV Sunday Talk Shows — such as *Meet the Press, State of the Union, Face the Nation, This Week,* and *Fox News Sunday,* who often have Overriding Conversations, whereby none of them can be Heard nor Understood, who get into Worthless Arguments without any Reasonable Solutions. First of all, they should have to Raise their Hands, just to get Permission to Speak, after being Recognized by some Host who is in Charge of the Talk Show, which would Eliminate some of that Noise and Confusion. ‡

13-14 [_] Well, they would naturally Argue that it would Break Up the Flow of all such Controversial Conversations, which might Diminish the Public Interest in it, which would be Bad for Business: beCause most People Like HOT Conversations, even as they Love Sword Fights and other Bloody Contests, which go all of the way back to the Days of the Gladiators, and the Contests in the Arenas — such as in the Colosseum / Coliseum in Rome, which was Located in the Temple of Peace part of Ancient Rome, even though it turned into a Place of Murder, Persecutions, and History knows what else. Lowlife Capitalists even Quarried Rocks from it, and others set up Sales Shops in it. It is still the largest Coliseum in the World, and gets more Visitors than any other Coliseum. The Problem with making a very Large Coliseum is the Fact that People can only See for certain Distances. For Example, try to Imagine Watching a Ball Game from a quarter of a Mile away, or even a half-mile away — how could you Enjoy it? Therefore, Gymnasiums should be Built like Theaters with Balconies: so as to make a Way for Spectators to be nearer to the Actors.

13-15 [_] O Elected King, I am not Satisfied with this Book about FAIR Swanky Wages, which have me Confused. Therefore, can you Summarize your Master Plan for us to Study?

— Chapter 14 —

A Summary of my Master Plan

14-01 [_] Money was no doubt Invented for the Convenience of Exchanging Goods and Services, which has Worked Well to some Degree for thousands of Years, while Dragging along with it no less than a Million Problems, whereby the Money Game has become so Complicated that Professional Economists cannot even Understand it, much less Control it, or make it Reliable and Trustworthy, even as a Swanky Fortress might be, which would be a Reliable Thing, even if the Rain should Stop: because of having Millions of Cisterns full of Fresh Water, even if we had to Distill Ocean Water to make Fresh Water, by putting that Distilled Water on Gardens, as if it were Pure Rainwater, whereby it would naturally run through the Topsoil, if it were in Excess of what the Garden might Use, and thus run into those Swanky Cisterns, according to my Plan that is Explained in: **"The LUSCIOUS All-Mineral Organic Method of Gardening!" (HOW to Grow DELICIOUS Satisfying Foods for Potential Kingz and Kweenz in Swanky PALACES!) By The Worldwide People's Revolution!® Book 021.**

14-02 [_] So, O Elected King, it seems that in your Economic System, above all others, there would be STABILITY: beCause, if the Gardens are Growing and Producing Foods, everyone would have a High Standard of Living: beCause of Living in those Swanky PALACES, which is as High as anyone's Standard of Living could get without Dying and going to Heaven, huh? †§‡

14-03 [_] Well, if almost everyone in the World has such a High Standard of Living, I cannot See HOW anyone could Improve on that Plan, can you? What would they Do to Improve on it — Sell Bubblegum and Balloons? Indeed, we can Live Healthy Happy Lives without any of the Capitalist Trash that one can now find for Sale, including those Stinking Noisy Polluting Cars, Pickups, Van, Trucks, Buses, Motorcycles, Lawnmowers, and so on — none of which were ever Needed for True Prosperity, which can easily be Proven in a Courtroom! However, if you Think that you cannot Live without Video Games, go ahead and have all of them that you Want, and it will not bother me, just as long as I have all of the Good Things that I Need to be Healthy and Happy, beginning with Fresh Clean Air, Pure Living Water, Wholesome Natural Foods, a Luscious All-Mineral Organic Garden that covers one whole Acre of Land, and a Secure Stone Dome Home Complex with 4 one-million-gallon Cisterns for Water Storage, whereby I can be Assured of Foods and Clothing and SECURITY, without Worrying about Terrorist Attacks, Robbers, Thieves, Liars, Deceivers, Betrayers of Trust, nor any of the Evil Creatures that have been Produced by Capitalism. ‡

14-04 [_] So, O Elected King, in your Economic System, if someone Needed some Extra Money for Buying a Mac Computer that has a 4-feet-wide Screen, that Person would only have to Work for more than 4 Hours of Common Labor per Day, and Save his Money, according to your List of FAIR Swanky Wages, which can be found in Chapter 08 Verse 08, huh? In other Words, after such a Person has put in his or her 4 Hours of Common Labor, he or she could do 2 or 3 more Hours of Work per Day, and Save as much Money as he or she might Earn by Honest Labor, without Borrowing any Money for Buying the Computer: beCause **"The New RIGHTEOUS One-World Government"** would Provide those Large Computers for whomever Wants them, and without Loaning any Money for Buying them, right?

14-05 [_] That is Correct for all Members of **"The Swanky Associations of Working Soldiers,"** who would Naturally be Trustworthy Honest People, who would Pay for such a Computer at Cost. For Example, if all of the Parts and Labor amount to 5,000$, then that would be the Cost of it. Moreover, it would be Designed to Endure the Test of Time, being Top-Quality Work, which would Belong to **"The New RIGHTEOUS One-World Government,"** until someone should make the Final Payment for it; and then it would be their Tool to use, give away, or do whatever they might Want to do with it, except to Trash it: beCause that Good Government would Buy it back, if they did not Want it any longer, which would be True for ALL Swanky Tools, which would have a Lifetime Guarantee on them. Therefore, you could Expect such a Computer to Endure no less than 100 Years, even if some Part had to be Replaced. Therefore, it would be Important to take Good Care of it, which Means that it must be Protected within some Swanky Stone Dome Home, where it is not in Danger of Burning Up, Blowing Away, nor being Buried during an Earthquake: beCause it is a very Valuable Tool, which would also most likely put out a LOT of HEAT, which would be the Primary Objection for having such Large Computer Screens: beCause it is the Nature of them, which would also be Drinking Up a LOT of Electricity. Therefore, I Suggest that everyone should be Contented with Small Computer Screens, which are 30-inches Wide, diagonally, from one Corner to another, which is a fairly large Screen. Indeed,

(The Equitable Wage System!)

we would Mass-produce those Computers for whomever might Want one, even though they also get fairly Hot; but, they make more Things Possible — such as Displaying several Websites at the same Time. However, normally-speaking, most People would be Contented with smaller Screens on their Computers. However, a large Screen has the Great Advantage of Showing LARGE Pictures, which could be Shown on their Large TV Screens, which could be 4 feet or more Wide, which would be Provided by **"The Swanky Association of Communications and Transportations!"** ‡

14-06 [_] So, O Elected King, according to your Master Plan, all of the Tools, TV's, Radios, Music Boxes, Telephones, Blenders, Stoves, Kitchens, Living Rooms, Bathrooms, Bedrooms, Swimming Pools, Pool Rooms, Game Rooms, and everything of Value would Belong to **"The New RIGHTEOUS One-World Government,"** until someone should Buy such Things, if they Wanted to Own them. Therefore, would those Tools and other Things not get OLD and Used-looking? Would the Computers be Updated, now and then: so as to be Equal to the Latest Model? Would all of the Kitchen Tools be First Class Quality: so as to be passed down from Generation to Generation, whereby the Great Great Grandchildren would not get to Enjoy any NEW Tools, TV's, Radios, Telephones, nor anything? †§‡

14-07 [_] Well, if the People were Discontented with their Swanky Tools, they could get Brand New ones. However, if such Tools are taken Good Care of, they will Endure for hundreds, if not thousands of Years, and still Look Good: beCause of being Gold-plated with Artistic Designs, if you Want such Things, and even be Diamond-studded: because there are LOTS of Diamonds in this World of Wonders. Therefore, the Important Thing is to come up with a Good Design, to begin with, which everyone can be Happy with. Moreover, there could be many Different Designs to Choose from, even if all of the "Guts" of the Computers are Exactly the same, whereby the Parts are Interchangeable with other Computers. Likewise, all Tools will be made to Endure the Test of Time, and have Replaceable Parts, if those Parts Wear Out, even as most Mechanical Things do: beCause of FRICTION, or Rubbing, even though we have a Bricklayer's Trowel that is more than 40 Years Old, which has been Used a LOT, and it is still in Good Shape: beCause it was made Correctly, back during the Good Old Days, when Americans Believed in Quality Products. No Modern Trowel is nearly as Good, as far as I know. ‡

14-08 [_] So, O Elected King, if all such Tools are made so Well, they will not be Wearing Out, nor be Thrown into the Trash Dump. Therefore, it will not be long before we Working Soldiers will have nothing to DO: beCause of Building those **"GLORIOUS Swanky Hotels Castles and Fortresses,"** which will also Endure the Test of Time, and thus we will all be Unemployed, just as soon as the Last Tile has been Set on the Last Wall. Therefore, HOW will we Obtain any more MONEY? †§‡

14-09 [_] Trust me, you will not Object to being Unemployed, once all of those **"Beautiful Swanky PALACES"** are Finished: because there will be Endless Things to Do, if you are Ambitious. Indeed, you are Free to DESIGN Eternal Employment, just by Building those Swanky CASTLES, which contain the Government Headquarters, the Court Houses, Offices, Thrones, Armories, Museums, Empty Jail Cells, Churches, Cathedrals, Basilicas, Temples, Mosques, Synagogues, Entertainment Centers, Schools, Universities, Special Shopping Mauls, and whatever you can Dream Up — that is, if you are not Contented to lean back in your Swanky Hand-carved Leather Easy Chair, and Play your Martin Guitar, Violin, or whatever you Like.

Otherwise, you could go Fishing, Hunting, Touring National Parks, Visiting other Swanky Fortresses, or just EAT; but, I Recommend that you do some Serious FASTING, whereby you might get Closer to GOD, who is All that is GOOD. Yes, you will then have Time to Explore the Spiritual Realm, and perhaps Converse with Holy Angels, if they find you Worthy of such Visitations. After all, when you get Hungry, you can always Visit a Royal Swanky Buffet, where you can Eat all of the Fresh Sweet Mangos that you might Want: beCause there will be an Abundance of Frozen Mangos in Walk-in Freezers, which make Perfect 100% Pure Mango Iced-cream — that is, IF **"The Swanky Association of Fruit Growers"** can get enough of them Planted and Growing and Producing, which will likely Require 10 Years or more: because Trees take TIME to Grow Up, being like Babies. Therefore, it is now Time to get them Planted by the BILLIONS, and only the Best of the Varieties, which Produce FRAGRANT Sweet Healthy Mangos, which Satisfy the Soul, which make you HAPPY just to Eat them, which are best Eaten without Touching your Teeth: beCause the Subtle Acids in them can Eat your Teeth. Therefore, Mango Ice-cream is the Right Way to Eat them, unless they are JUICED, or made into Smoothies with other Exotic Fruits. ‡

14-10 [_] So, O Elected King of the Mountain, it Sounds like a True Economy has Endless Employment, until all of those **"GLORIOUS Swanky Hotels Castles and Fortresses"** are Finished, and then everyone will be on a Long Swanky VACATION, huh? Will that be the Great Year of JUBILEE? Will we be Occupying our Time with Parades and other Government Nonsense? Will we be Ordered about like SLAVES, or what?

14-11 [_] Well, you may be Invited to Participate in Parades. For Example, one Swanky Fortress may put on a Parade for another Swanky Fortress, who may Exchange Parades, whenever they Want to Show Off their Beauty or whatever they have to Offer. After all, there will be Countless Flower Gardens within Swanky Fortresses, which will be Attended to by **"The Swanky Association of Flower Gardeners!"** Therefore, they could make Colorful Floats for Parades, much like the Pasadena Tournament of Roses Parade, in Californicate, only much more Artistic: beCause of not being Limited by a Lack of Money, if they are Willing to Earn it. After all, there will be many Ways to Earn those GOOD Swanky Wages. Besides that, the Flowers will be Free of Charge, and may even be Donated and Delivered by that same Association. Moreover, there will be many Home-craft Workshops that will be Producing New and Marvelous Things to Sell, including Ceramic Flower Pots with Special Designs, which will Enhance many Walkways, whereby those **"GLORIOUS Swanky Hotels Castles and Fortresses"** will become Tourist Attractions like you have never Seen, which Tourists may be Limited to Visiting the Hotels and Castles, only: beCause the People who Live within the Fortresses might not Want so many Visitors Roaming all about. However, they might Watch for Special Visitors on TV Channels that Show them Entering into the Hotels, whereby they might Want to Contact those Special Visitors, and Invite them to Visit them, in Person. After all, it will be a Lover's Paradise! ‡

14-12 [_] So, O Elected King, will those Swanky Fortresses not also become Grand Temptations for all Young People, who will be Lusting after those Beautiful Visitors at the Swanky Hotels? Indeed, such Young Healthy People will be Irresistible to other Healthy Young People, who will no doubt be Committing Adultery with those Visitors. ‡

14-13 [_] Well, there is the Danger of that, for Sure; but, everyone will be Encouraged to Practice FIDELITY, which is Faithfulness to just one other Person, which is Good. Therefore, to

(The Equitable Wage System!)

Avoid Adultery and Fornication, it is Best for everyone to be Married, who can Discover Life Mates by simply Filling Out and Filing **"The Complete SURVEYS of our VALUES!" (SURVEYS of Religious Spiritual Political Governmental Sexual Social Moral Economic Business Labor Habitual and Miscellaneous VALUES!) By The Worldwide People's Revolution!® Book 059.** Yes, those Visitors may become Good Friends; but, not Lovers: because all of the Lovers can be Discovered before we even Build one Swanky Hotel, which will Eliminate a lot of Problems, and Stabilize Families, and Eliminate Divorces. ‡

14-14 [_] O Elected King, that seems to be Wishful Thinking, to me: beCause I Understand the Nature of People who Travel a lot, who seem to be Lusting after something, which they have not yet gotten, and especially if they are Single. Therefore, no Single People should be Allowed to take Swanky Vacations, alone, to Swanky Fortresses: because they are likely to get into Troubles, if not get Raped. †§‡

14-15 [_] Well, it would be their Decisions to make, since everyone would be Free, just as long as they Obey the Laws, which will not be that Difficult to Do: beCause, if they Want to Fornicate, for Example, there will be Swanky Fortresses that Permit it. Therefore, they only have to Visit those Fortresses. Therefore, I Suggest that all Young People should Fill Out and File the Surveys of their Values, whereby they might Discover other People of Like-mindedness, and thus be most Happy with them, which will be a New Experiment in World History, which will Prove certain Things that Need to be Proven. For Example, would White People Willingly Choose to Marry Black People, if they could Choose the Persons that they Actually Want to Marry? Or, do they Marry such People for the Sake of Lusts, Rebellion, Defiance, Greed, Selfishness, or what? It would be Interesting to Learn just how much LOVE was Involved in such Marriages, which often Produce very Unhappy Suicidal Children. ‡

— Chapter 15 —

The Conclusion

15-01 [_] Now, as you can See, we are coming to the End of this Inspired Book, which is Naturally Rejected by Unbelievers, who do not Want to Sacrifice their Greed, nor Selfishness, on the Altar of Truths, whereby they might Discover a much Better Way to Live, by United Effort with other Humble Honest Working Soldiers, who have all to Gain, and nothing to Lose, just by their Cooperation, which will, of course, Require MUCH Hard Work. However, when that Hard Work is Divided among 2 Billion Young Working Soldiers, Worldwide, who have the Correct Heavy Equipment to Work with, it suddenly seems to be very Light Easy Work. In Fact, if we get those **"Seven Great Armies of Working Soldiers"** Properly Organized, they will be able to Pump Out those **"GLORIOUS Swanky Hotels Castles and Fortresses,"** like Sausages from a Meat Grinder, which are Spiced and Ready to Hang Up in the Smoke House, in one Continuous Operation, you might say. Yes, the Foundations must first be Built with HUGE Concrete Cisterns for Water Storage, in order to LEVEL the Beautiful Planned City State, and to Raise it

Up above the Surrounding Terrain, which is often Located in a Swampy Place. Secondly, the Outermost Moat must then be Built, which will Keep Out any Unwanted Creatures, while also making a Good Water Storage Tank, you might say. Thirdly, there must be more Cisterns Built on Top of the Foundation Cisterns, inside of the Enclosed Area, which Cisterns must have Subway Tunnels for Electric Trains to run between the Cisterns, with Elevators, Escalators, and Granite Stairways to get to the Trains. Fourthly, each Tier of Cisterns must be Capped with a Flat Floor, in order to provide a Place to Build Stone Dome Home Complexes, and without using any Metals in the Concrete: because such Metals would only Rust Out and Weaken the Walls, which should all be 10 to 20 feet THICK, being Joined with Stone Barrel-vault Tunnels between Domes, even as I have already Described within **"The Right Design for Living!" (A List of Great Advantages for Building Beautiful Planned City States!) By The Worldwide People's Revolution!®** Book 012. Indeed, the whole City must be built in Great Terraces, like Steps that are 60 feet Tall, if the Living Room Domes are 40 feet Tall. (Some Wise People will Choose to make Domes no larger than 24 feet Wide and 20 feet Tall, having Vertical Walls that are 8 feet Tall, with True Domes on Top of them for Maximum Strength. However, even if those Domes were somewhat Flattened Out, and only 16 feet Tall in the Centers of them, they would be very Strong: because of being so THICK, and having Skylight Holes in the Tops of them, which are Cylindrical Shafts that reach up through the Rough Granite Rocks, Gravel, Sand, Clay, Sand, Gravel, Rough Rocks, Gravel, Sand, thicker Clay, Gravel, Sand, Subsoil, and Topsoil 3 feet Deep. Yes, it is Layered like that to put the Spooks in any Bombs that might be Dropped on such Stone Dome Home Complexes by Greedy Bloodthirsty Red Jews, who have Invented such Abominations as Atomic and Hydrogen Bombs. Entranceways can be Blocked with Solid Granite Rocks that are 10 feet Thick, just to Keep Out those "Smart Bombs," if we cannot Persuade all Nations to get RID of all such Abominations.) ‡

15-02 [_] O Elected King, could we not Save ourselves a LOT of Hard Work, just by getting RID of those Abominations, before Building any Swanky Hotels, Castles and Fortresses? After all, there is no Good Reason for Trying to make all such Fortresses BOMB-PROOF, even though they should be Terrorist-proof. After all, you probably Remember how the Allies dropped no less than 50,000 Tons of Bombs on the German Bunkers, at Normandy, and they never Managed to Knock Out even ONE German Bunker, none of which had 20 feet or more Rocks, Gravel, Sand, Clay, and whatever on the Roofs of them, as you Propose. Indeed, such Bombs would no doubt mess up the Organic Gardens; but, they would have Zero Effects on those Stone Dome Homes, which would have Roofs that are no less than 10 feet THICK, made of Hardened Concrete and Covered with Granite Rocks. Indeed, such Bombs would only Bounce Off of such Hard Stone Domes. †§‡

15-03 [_] Well, you might Think that, as would a lot of Ignorant People; but, those Red Jews have figured out how to have 2 or 3 Bombs following the first Bomb, which makes a Path for the other Bombs to follow; but, only at a Great Expense: because no such Bombs are Cheap. Indeed, they call them Bunker-busting Bombs, which are Designed for Deep Penetrations into Mountains and Bunkers. Some of them weigh as much or more than 30,000 Pounds, and are Dropped from 20,000 or more feet up in the Sky, with an Accuracy of plus or minus 23 feet. Therefore, just to be Safe, all Swanky Fortresses would have to be Covered with very Hard Steel a foot Thick, just to Weaken their Blows, which Steel Sheets would have to be Covered with Spikes that are 3 feet Long, which are Designed to Pierce through the Nose Cones of the Bombs, and Cause them to EXPLODE before Penetrating the foot-thick Steel Sheets, and thus Penetrating into the Organic

(The Equitable Wage System!)

Gardens. However, when such Bombs are falling at such Rapid Speeds, it is presumed that X-amount of their Parts would Penetrate through the Steel Sheets, and also through the Topsoil, Subsoil, Sand, Gravel, Clay, Sand, Gravel, Clay, large Rough Rocks, and all of the way down to a Swanky Stone Dome Home, which could also be Covered with another foot of Hardened Steel Sheets with Sand between the Sheets, in 2 or 3 Layers: so as to make them somewhat Bomb-resistant, before the Bomb Penetrated to the Solid Stone Dome Home, whereby it would only Bounce Off, after Hitting a Springboard, which is Designed for making it Bounce and Explode in Midair. †§‡§§

15-04 [_] O Elected King, it does seem like we Desperately Need to Establish **"The New RIGHTEOUS One-World Government,"** whereby all such Hateful Weapons can be Destroyed, and then will not have to Waste so many Materials on Swanky Stone Dome Homes. ‡

15-05 [_] Well, that is exactly what I have been saying for more than 30 Years! After all, I do not know of one single American Family who is so Well Protected, right now, do you? Indeed, it seems that they are all Vulnerable to much less Deadly Weapons, and even Bullets from Rifles.

15-06 [_] So, O Elected King, Knowing for a FACT that very few Enemies would have the Resources for Producing any such Big Bombs, it seems to be Reasonable to Think that just a Normal Swanky Fortress, which has 20 feet of Rocks and Dirt on Top of the Domes, would be Sufficient to Deter 99.99% of the Bombs that might be Delivered on them. After all, even without the Steel Spikes and thick Steel Sheets, no such Bombs would have any Effects on the Domes that are 3 or 4 Floors BELOW the Surface Domes: beCause that would Require Bombs no less than 200,000 Pounds, which no Airplane could Lift. Therefore, they would have to be Fired by Rocket Launchers, and Controlled like Guided Missiles, which would Cost several Billion dollars, just for one of them. Therefore, bringing Down a Swanky Fortress that has Millions of Stone Domes would be Extremely Difficult, if not Impossible. Moreover, nothing would be Gained by it: beCause all of those People could be Evacuated to another Swanky Fortress, by using Underground Railways, which are Protected by a hundred feet of Granite Rocks on Top of them, being under Forests, being Totally Hidden from View of anything. Indeed, what are the Chance of Defeating **"The New RIGHTEOUS One-World Government"** with little Bombs?

15-07 [_] Well, the Subways in London, England, are supposed to be 200 feet below the Ground Level, which they used for Air Raid Shelters during World War 2. None of them were Damaged, as far as I know. However, those Tunnels were not Designed for People to Live in them, which had very Bad Air in them.

15-08 [_] So, O Elected King, it Sounds like we could Save TRILLIONS of Dollars, just by Establishing **"The New RIGHTEOUS One-World Government!"** Therefore, what would we Spend the Money on, if there are no more Wars, no more Bankers, no more Interest on Loans, no more Expensive Drugs, no more Capitalist Medical Doctors, no Wicked Greedy Lawyers, no Politicians, no Lying Preachers, no Charity Organizations, no Insurance Agents, and no other Capitalist Thieves, Liars, Robbers, nor even Weekly Tabloids for Sale?

15-09 [_] Well, when all of the Debts are Forgiven, there will not even be any Need for Paying Off those Debts. Therefore, it looks like we will have to just Sit on our Money, since everyone who Wants a Diamond Ring can have one on each Finger, if it will make them Feel Important enough to be Honest.

15-10 [_] O Elected King, it does seem like Life could be a lot more Simple, and People could be a lot more Innocent, and would be so, if they were Born and Raised in those **"GLORIOUS Swanky Hotels Castles and Fortresses!" (Beautiful Planned City States for WISE Intelligent Well-Educated People with Common Sense and Good Understanding!) By The Worldwide People's Revolution!**® Book 019. Indeed, just those Luscious All-Mineral Organic Gardens, alone, would have a Tendency to make People more Godly and Humane, and especially if their Hateful Songs and Evil Video Games were taken away from them, and put into the same Trash Dump with those Radioactive Bombs, and other Abominations on the Planet of the Apes. †§‡

15-11 [_] Well, that is what I Tried to Explain in my Inspired Book, called: **"Poverty Hunger Riots Strikes Brutalities Election Deceptions and Civil Wars!" (The High Price that we Earthlings have Paid for Leaving the Good Land!) By The Worldwide People's Revolution!**® Book 014. Indeed, the many Problems that Plague the Urbanites are no Problems for the Old Order Mennonites, Amish, Hutterites, and other Peoples who Live on the Land, and Attend to their Animals and Crops, who keep their Minds Centered on Better Things than Selling Drugs and Raping Women. ‡

15-12 [_] O Elected King, I do Wish to God that I had been Born into a Family like your own, whereby I might have had some Common Sense, and could Think. After all, I was Greatly Deceived by that Public School of Ignorant Fools, who wanted to get me Lined Up to become another Capitalist Tax Slave, Interest Slave, Insurance Slave, Drug Slave, Childcare Slave, Sex Slave, and Work Slave, just like 99.99% of all other Americans, who have no Idea what it Means to be Free with a Capital F, like you. ‡

15-13 [_] Well, if I had not been Free for the past 45 Years, I could not have Accomplished all of the Good Things that I have Accomplished, including my 350+ Inspired Books, which are my Greatest Achievements: beCause they have the Potential of Changing the World for the Better, which would be very Good. However, it cannot Happen, if People do not Buy and Read the Books.

15-14 [_] O King of the Birds, this is certainly not your Best Book; but, it is certainly Worthy to be "red" by whomever likes to "reed." Moreover, I Promise to do whatever I can to Encourage other People to read your Fascinating Books: beCause they are Inspiring and Uplifting. Indeed, they give to me a lot of HOPE that I did not used to have.

15-15 [_] Well, if you Want a LOT of Hope, I Recommend that you Study: **"The New MAGNIFIED Version of The Book of MOORMUN!" (The Story of the White and Dark Indians in the Americas!) By The Worldwide People's Revolution!**® Book 040, which comes in 2 large Volumes of about 500 pages each. Be sure to read the Description on Amazon.com, which Reveals HOW to Obtain both Volumes of that Good Book for "FREE"! Actually, it will be Paid for by the Church of Jesus Christ of Latter-day Sinners.

(The Equitable Wage System!)

— Chapter 16 —

A "Long Boring List" of other Fascinating Books by the same Inspired Author!

16-001 [_] "LIGHTNING Versus the Lightning Bug!" (HOW almost Everyone can become Moderately RICH, without Telling Any Lies nor Selling Any Trash!) By The Worldwide People's Revolution!® Book 001. The Cover Photo shows a Beautiful Sunrise in the Blest Land of Eternal Springtime!

16-002 [_] "What is WRong with those Professing Christians?" (A Self-Examination of the Heart of the Body of Good Government!) By The Worldwide People's Revolution!® Book 002. The Cover Photo shows a Small Portion of our Unfinished Retirement Home.

16-003 [_] "For the Love of Money!" (The Strange Things that People Say and Do to Get more Money!) By The Worldwide People's Revolution!® Book 003. The Cover Photo shows a Jewish Boy studying the *Scriptures.*

16-004 [_] "HOW to Prepare for CLIMATE CHANGES!" (The Wisest Plan for Mankind to Follow!) By The Worldwide People's Revolution!® Book 004. The Cover Photo shows Dark Awesome Clouds.

16-005 [_] "WHY do I have to be Surrounded by CRAZY PEOPLE?" (Do almost all People Feel like they are Surrounded by CRAZY PEOPLE??) By The Worldwide People's Revolution!® Book 005. The Cover Photo shows Delicious Fragrant Ripe Mangos.

16-006 [_] "The Washington Journal is a FARCE!" (C-SPAN Managers are not very WISE!) By The Worldwide People's Revolution!® Book 006. The Cover Photo shows a Portion of "Mars," up close.

16-007 [_] "The PRAYERS of PUMPKINHEADS!" (Even God Needs a Little Humor to Cheer himself Up!) By The Worldwide People's Revolution!® Book 007. The Cover Photo shows the Author's Brother standing beside a very large Tree in the Blest Land of Eternal Springtime.

16-008 [_] "A Sound Argument for Masters and Servants!" (WHY Everyone Needs a Good Master, and every Master Needs Good Obedient Servants!) By The Worldwide People's Revolution!® Book 008. The Cover Photo shows a Pleasant Manmade Waterfalls.

16-009 [_] "WHY are some Preachers so POOR?" (HOW almost all Preachers could Get RICH, without Preaching any Outlandish LIES!) By The Worldwide People's Revolution!® Book 009. The Cover Photo shows a Portion of the Inside of a Gold-laden Church in the Blest Land of Eternal Springtime, worth a Billion Dollars!

16-010 [_] "GOOD NEWS for REBEL WOMEN!" (HOW almost all Wives can become Moderately Rich without Leaving their Homes! Guaranteed!) By The Worldwide People's Revolution!® Book 010. The Cover Photo shows Beautiful Ceramic Work in the Blest Land of Eternal Springtime.

16-011 [_] "The Low Court of Supreme Injustices is Brought to Trial!" (The Worldwide People's Revolution Butts Heads with the United States Supreme Court, with or without their Black Robes of Hypocrisies and Lies!) By The Worldwide People's Revolution!® Book 011. The Cover Photo shows the United States Supreme Court Building in Washington.

16-012 [_] "The Right Design for Living!" (A List of Great Advantages for Building Beautiful Planned City States!) By The Worldwide People's Revolution!® Book 012. The Cover Photo shows the Great Pyramid at Chichen Itza, in Mexico.

16-013 [_] "The Gospel According to The Worldwide People's Revolution!" (The Good News from the Most Modern Perspective!) By The Worldwide People's Revolution!® Book 013. The Cover Photo shows a very Dirty Drunkard lying by the Street in the Cursed Land of Childish Rebellion, which does not Believe in Righteous Kings.

16-014 [_] "Poverty Hunger Riots Strikes Brutalities Election Deceptions and Civil Wars!" (The High Price that we Earthlings have Paid for Leaving the Good Land!) By The Worldwide People's Revolution!® Book 014. The Cover Photo shows Tombs in a Cemetery.

16-015 [_] "Seven Great Armies of Working Soldiers!" (HOW to Provide a Way for Everyone to WORK: so as to Eliminate Poverty, Crimes, Drug Abuses, Prisons and Unnecessary Taxes!) By The Worldwide People's Revolution!® Book 015. The Cover Photo shows a Truckload of Potential Working Soldiers.

16-016 [_] "The CONSTITUTION for the New RIGHTEOUS One-World GovernMint!" (HOW all Peoples can get True Justice, and Celebrate the Great Year of JUBILEE!) By The Worldwide People's Revolution!® Book 016. The Cover Photo shows a Gathering Thunderstorm.

16-017 [_] "The Great World TEMPLE of PEACE!" (The Glory of Jerusalem Arises Again!) By The Worldwide People's Revolution!® Book 017. The Cover Photo shows Old Jerusalem in all of its Naked and Potential Glory.

16-018 [_] "The Swanky Associations of Working Soldiers!" (A Fascinating Collection of Various Kinds of Voluntary Working Soldiers!) By The Worldwide People's Revolution!® Book 018. The Cover Photo shows a Beautiful Malachite Pyramid.

16-019 [_] "GLORIOUS Swanky Hotels Castles and Fortresses!" (Beautiful Planned City States for WISE Intelligent Well-Educated People with Common Sense and Good Understanding!) By The Worldwide People's Revolution!® Book 019. The Cover Photo shows a Beautiful "Million-dollar" Onyx Box in all of its Naked Glory.

(The Equitable Wage System!)

16-020 [_] "Are you a Jobless Graduate of the SKQL uv FQLZ?" (HOW to Get a GOUD EJUKAASHUN without Robbing the Bank!) By The Worldwide People's Revolution!® Book 020. The Cover Photo shows a small and Beautiful Onyx Vase.

16-021 [_] "The LUSCIOUS All-Mineral Organic Method of Gardening!" (HOW to Grow DELICIOUS Satisfying Foods for Potential Kingz and Kweenz in Swanky PALACES!) By The Worldwide People's Revolution!® Book 021. The Cover Photo shows Beautiful Green Terraces in the Blest Land of Eternal Summertime.

16-022 [_] "Did God or Satan Ordain Medical Doctors??" (Ask Huck Finn and/or Nigger Jim: because neither Tom Sawyer nor Judge Thatcher would Know!) By The Worldwide People's Revolution!® Book 022. The Cover Photo shows Pretty Flowers at a Tomb.

16-023 [_] "The BIG White OUTHOUSE on the Not-so-Biblical Capitol DUNGHILL!" (The Chief Sins of the Divided States of United Lies!) By The Worldwide People's Revolution!® Book 023. The Cover Photo shows the Capitol Building in Washington, District of Criminals, District of Confusion, District of Colombian Drug Addicts, etc., etc.

16-024 [_] "The Public School of IGNERUNT FQLZ!" (HOW we have been GRAATLEE DISEEVD!) By The Worldwide People's Revolution!® Book 024. The Cover Photo shows a Disorganized Fruit Market in a City of Confusion.

16-025 [_] "In thu Beeginingz uv Thingz!" (Thu Kreeaashun Stooree frum thu Beegining!) By The Worldwide People's Revolution!® Book 025. The Cover Photo shows a Yellow Sapote, which not one Person in a Million has ever Tasted, in spite of being one of the most Pleasant Sweetest Fruits known to Mankind, which does not Ship very well, which must Ripen on the Tree, in order to be Extremely GOOD, as in "Heavenly Good!"

16-026 [_] "God Speaks and the Whole World Listens!" (Fire on the Mountain from the Burning Bush by the Spirit of Truth!) By The Worldwide People's Revolution!® Book 026. The Cover Photo shows the Sign or Flag for **"The New RIGHTEOUS One-World Government!"**

16-027 [_] "Does a Good Soldier have to be a MURDERER?" (Seven Great Swanky Armies of Voluntary Working Soldiers!) By The Worldwide People's Revolution!® Book 027. Dan.

16-028 [_] "Thu Nq MAGNUFIID Verzhun uv Thu PROVERBZ uv KING SOLUMUN in Plaan Ingglish!" (The Understandable Version of the Famous Proverbs of King Solomon in Plain English!) By The Worldwide People's Revolution!® Book 028. The Cover Photo shows Gemstones in an Onyx Jewelry Box.

16-029 [_] "UNLIMITED ENERJEE 99 Percent Pollutions Free!" (HOW to Obtain FREE ElecTrickery, Worldwide!) By The Worldwide People's Revolution!® Book 029. The Cover Photo shows an Onyx Tray for a large Spoon in the Kitchen.

16-030 [_] "FREEDUM uv SPEECH!" (U Speshoul Maguzeen uv Onust Upinyunz!) By The Worldwide People's Revolution!® Book 030-0001. The Cover Photo shows a Portion of

107

one of the Author's Marble Countertops, worth 100$ per square foot, for an Example of what you could also have, if you Exercise your Faith, Hope, Trust, Love, Patience, Persistence, and OBEDIENCE!

16-031 [_] **"A Sure Cure for GUN VIOLENCE!" (HOW TO STOP GANG WARS and CRIMINAL SHOOTINGS!) By The Worldwide People's Revolution!®** Book 031. The Cover Photo shows a Short Shotgun, which is fully loaded and ready for any Tax Master who might Attempt to Steel the Retirement Home, who never moved a Finger to Help Build it, whose Anti-Christ False Federal Cover-up WICKED Government allowed Banksters to Rob us of 30 Years of Hard Work and 300,000+ dollars-worth of Investments in our Uncommon American Farm. (Future Books will have Cover Photos of some of that Hard Work. Please be Patient.)

16-032 [_] **"AIIRMWVC and Reasonable Solutions!" (Aliens, Illegal Immigrants, Refugees, Migrant Workers and other Victims of Capitalism!) By The Worldwide People's Revolution!®** Book 032. The Cover Photo shows a "Sea of People."

16-033 [_] **"Mark Twain Races for the PRESIDENCY!" (The 2016 Presidential Candidates Desperately Need Some STRONG Undefeatable COMPETITION!) By The Worldwide People's Revolution!®** Book 033. The Cover Photo shows a Mountain Goat and a Silver Dollar.

16-034 [_] **"ECCLESIASTES UNCOVERED!" (The New MAGNIFIED Version of Ecclesiastes and the Song of Solomon in Plain English!) By The Worldwide People's Revolution!®** Book 034. The Cover Photo shows a Peacock Resting.

16-035 [_] **"The Environmentalists' Paradise!" (HOW almost Everyone could be Living in a Beautiful Manmade Paradise!) By The Worldwide People's Revolution!®** Book 035. The Cover Photo shows an Artist's Conception of Paradise for a single Family in the Blest Land of Perfect Oneness, where all is at Peace.

16-036 [_] **"The Seven Basic Spiritual Building Blocks of LIFE!" (Faith Hope Trust Love Patience Persistence and Obedience!) By The Worldwide People's Revolution!®** Book 036. The Cover Photo shows Onion Domes trimmed with Gold.

16-037 [_] **"DIETS!" (A Reasonable Solution for the "Eternal Controversy"!) By The Worldwide People's Revolution!®** Book 037. The Cover Photo shows some Colorful Fruits.

16-038 [_] **"The Nature of CAPITALISM!" (A List of the EVILS of CAPITALISM!) By The Worldwide People's Revolution!®** Book 038. The Cover Photo shows a Pretty Red Car.

16-039 [_] **"SWANGKEENOMIKS Rules the Roost!" (HOW all People can Prosper in a RIIT WAA, and STOP Polluting the Earth with Capitalist TRASH!) By The Worldwide People's Revolution!®** Book 039. The Cover Photo shows a small Portion of our Retirement Home before the 5,000+ square-foot Roof was Installed.

16-040 [_] **"The New MAGNIFIED Version of The Book of MOORMUN!" (The Story of the White and Dark Indians in the Americas!) By The Worldwide People's Revolution!®** Book 040, Volumes 1 and 2. The Cover Photos show the Queen of England's Golden Coach, and

(The Equitable Wage System!)

one of our Marbleous Spanish Walls, which is worth a thousand dollars per square Yard, installed on 7 similar Walls, which are 12 feet long. It is very Inspiring. No one could Study it for very long without Believing in a Great Creator God.

16-041 [_] "The Great Worldwide TELEVISED Court HEARING!" (That Great Meeting of the Most Intelligent Minds!) By The Worldwide People's Revolution!® Book 041. The Cover Photo shows Mount Popotits covered with Snow.

16-042 [_] "The Secret City of the Great King!" (HOW the True Church will Escape from the Great Tribulation!) By The Worldwide People's Revolution!® Book 042. The Cover Photo shows a Colorful Ferris Wheel. P-5877.

16-043 [_] "Terrorists Beware that your Days are Numbered!" (HOW to Bring those Terrorist Attacks to a Screeching HALT!) By The Worldwide People's Revolution!® Book 043. The Cover Photo shows a Picture of George Warmonger Bush. This Book also contains the Fascinating Book of LEHI.

16-044 [_] "The New MAGNIFIED Version of ISAIAH in Plain English!" (The Understandable Version of the Book of Isaiah!) By The Worldwide People's Revolution!® Book 044. The Cover Photo shows a Swanky Potato / Avocado Salad with Sweet Peas and Corn.

16-045 [_] "HOW to Become a HOLY Man!" (40 Good Reasons WHY People Should FAST and PRAY!) By The Worldwide People's Revolution!® Book 045. The Cover Photo will show a Holy Man, just as soon as one Presents himself for the Photograph.

16-046 [_] "The Proper RULES for FASTING!" (The Complete Instruction Manual for True Repentance!) By The Worldwide People's Revolution!® Book 046. The Cover Photo shows an Unclean Man.

16-047 [_] "Are Americans the Most STUPID People who ever Lived?" (HOW Working People can PROSPER and Live in PEACE Under the Rulership of a RIGHTEOUS KING!) By The Worldwide People's Revolution!® Book 047. The Cover Photo shows a large Portion of the Author's Marbleous Living Room Floor, which is worth 100,000$.

16-048 [_] "An Amazing Collection of Wit and Wisdom!" (The Marvelous Tale of the Colorful Peacock from Angel Ridge, and the Strong Rope of Hope!) By The Worldwide People's Revolution!® Book 048. The Cover Photo shows a Book Display.

16-049 [_] "Justifications for Capitalizations!" (WHY The Worldwide People's Revolution!® Defies the School of Fools by Capitalizing Love and Hate!) By The Worldwide People's Revolution!® Book 049. The Cover Photo shows a Water Tower.

16-050 [_] "The END of CONFUSION!" (The Great CELEBRATION of the Magnificent Wedding of the Humble Honest Nations, and the Grand Year of JUBILEE!) By The Worldwide People's Revolution!® Book 050. The Cover Photo shows a Portion of a Colorful Parade.

A List of FAIR Swanky Wages!

16-051 [_] "The Loathsome Burdens of the Independent Jackasses!" (A New Approach for Solving our Massive Problems!) By The Worldwide People's Revolution!® Book 051. The Cover Photo shows a Spanish Military Barracks.

16-052 [_] "Are we Tax Slaves of a Lower Order than Lying Red JEWS?" (HOW to be Liberated from all Slavery, Worldwide!) By The Worldwide People's Revolution!® Book 052. The Cover Photo shows a few Tax Slaves.

16-053 [_] "The Great False Economy is now DEBUNKED!" (Adolf Hitler had a much Better Economic System!) By The Worldwide People's Revolution!® Book 053. The Cover Photo shows a Capitalist Toilet Brush.

16-054 [_] "The UGLY Scarred Dishonest Face of Poor Old Miserable UNCLE SAM!" (A Memorial Day Legacy!) By The Worldwide People's Revolution!® Book 054. The Cover Photo shows a Poster of "Uncle Sam," who Symbolizes the Federal Government of **"The Divided States of United Lies!"**

16-055 [_] "The United States of the Whole World!" (A True Global Economy for the Masses of Working People!) By The Worldwide People's Revolution!® Book 055. A Photo of a 110-year-old Well-made Mexican Rocking Chair with a Cowhide Seat.

16-056 [_] "The New RIGHTEOUS One-World Government!" (HOW to Establish a Righteous One-World Government without Going to WAR!) By The Worldwide People's Revolution!® Book 056. The Cover Photo shows the Flag of that Good Government.

16-057 [_] "Those Ridiculous Contradictions within the Holy Bible!" (HOW to Read the Bible with an Open Mind!) By The Worldwide People's Revolution!® Book 057. The Cover Photo shows a Purple Tree.

16-058 [_] "The Divided States of United Lies!" (The so-called "United States of North America," in Disguise!) By The Worldwide People's Revolution!® Book 058. The Cover Photo shows a Map of the United States.

16-059 [_] "The Complete SURVEYS of our VALUES!" (SURVEYS of Religious Spiritual Political Governmental Sexual Social Moral Economic Business Labor Habitual and Miscellaneous VALUES! By The Worldwide People's Revolution!® Book 059. The Cover Photo shows a Large Onyx Vase in the Author's Palace.

16-060 [_] "HOW to Get our PRIORITIES in ORDER!" (The Glories of Democracy; and, Does DEMON-ocracy have its Priorities in Order?) By The Worldwide People's Revolution!® Book 060. The Cover Photo shows a Different View of that Large Onyx Vase.

16-061 [_] "The New MAGNIFIED Version of the GOOD NEWS According to Saint LUKE!" (The Magnified Gospel of Luke in Plain English!) By The Worldwide People's Revolution!® Book 061. The Cover Photo shows Agate Windows.

16-062 [_] "The New MAGNIFIED Version of the GOOD NEWS According to Saint JOHN!" (The Gospel According to Saint John Zebedee Boanerges in Plain English!) By The Worldwide People's Revolution!® Book 062. The Cover Photo shows the Parthenon.

16-063 [_] "The New MAGNIFIED Version of the Book of ACTS!" (The Understandable Version of the ACTS of the Apostles in Plain English!) By The Worldwide People's Revolution!® Book 063. The Cover Photo shows a Small Portion of Arches National Park.

16-064 [_] "The New MAGNIFIED Version of the PSALMS of King David!" (The Understandable Version of the Famous Psalms in Plain English!) By The Worldwide People's Revolution!® Book 064. The Cover Photo shows some of the Grand Canyon.

16-065 [_] "A List of FAIR Swanky Wages!" (The Equitable Wage System!) By The Worldwide People's Revolution!® Book 065. The Cover Photo shows a Pile of Money.

16-066 [_] "Beautiful Swanky PALACES!" (A New Concept in Living Habits — Palaces for Poor People!) By The Worldwide People's Revolution!® Book 066. The Cover Photo shows a Bouquet of Pretty Flowers in the Author's Kitchen.

16-067 [_] "The Swanky Sword of Divine Truths!" (The Most Powerful Weapon in the Whole Universe!) By The Worldwide People's Revolution!® Book 067.

{NOTE: This List of Available Books will be Updated Periodically. If you fail to find any of these Books on Amazon.com, just be Patient: because I am a One-Man Army, you might say. All of the Books are written, and just need to be Posted, after they are Updated.}

And you were Thinking that Minimum Wages should be at least 15$ per Hour, huh? Well, **The Worldwide People's Revolution!®** Radically Disagrees with such Low Wages with a Capital R and D: beCause there is no Justice in it with a Capital J, as Jesus Christ might Pay, who Believed in Fairness with a Capital B and F, even as you can Discover for yourself in the Unholy Mutilated Bible, which is Missing a very Important Quotation that can be Found in this Inspired Book, which comes from the Gospel According to Saint Bartholomew, which Reveals HOW to Obtain the True Riches! However, there are also other Necessary Material Riches, which should be Obtainable by Honest Labor, without making yourself a Slave of anyone, much less an Eternal Tax Slave, Interest Slave, Insurance Slave, Drug Slave, Debt Slave, Childcare Slave, and WORK SLAVE, even as most Silly Americans have done: beCause of their IGNORANCE! Yes, Shame on them; but, Double Shame on you, if you Disregard the Provable Truths that are Found within this Inspired Book, which Reveals HOW to get the Best Wages in the World, which are SWANKY WAGES! Guaranteed!

www.ingramcontent.com/pod-product-compliance
Lightning Source LLC
Chambersburg PA
CBHW080705190526

45169CB00006B/2253